IN SEARCH OF CIVILITY:

Confronting Incivility on the College Campus

KENT M. WEEKS, Ph.D AND J.D.

NEW YORK

IN SEARCH OF CIVILITY
Confronting Incivility on the College Campus

by **KENT M. WEEKS, Ph.D AND J.D.**
© 2011 Kent M. Weeks. All rights reserved.

ISBN 978-1-60037-907-9 (paperback)

Published by:

MORGAN JAMES PUBLISHING
The Entrepreneurial Publisher
5 Penn Plaza, 23rd Floor
New York City, New York 10001
(212) 655-5470 Office
(516) 908-4496 Fax
www.MorganJamesPublishing.com

Interior Design by:
Bonnie Bushman

In an effort to support local communities, raise awareness and funds, Morgan James Publishing donates one percent of all book sales for the life of each book to Habitat for Humanity.
Get involved today, visit
www.HelpHabitatForHumanity.org.

ACKNOWLEDGMENTS

Many people contributed to *In Search of Civility*. The colleges and universities with whom I work care deeply about developing a climate of civility and over the years have raised interesting questions regarding the appropriate role of colleges in nurturing a caring community on campus. My students, who lead incredibly busy lives, helped me to see the complexity of the issues through their eyes.

In addition, many others contributed in significant and specific ways. While finishing up his legal studies, my student assistant Aaron Chastain, shaped the scenarios of the four students profiled in the book, conveying issues both pointed and nuanced. Ernie Gilkes, my paralegal, contributed new ideas and analyses and provided research assistance and technical support. My children who teach undergraduate students and their spouses encouraged me not to underestimate the ability of students to do the right thing and offered some ideas about design of the cover of the book. Finally, my wife, Karen, provided editorial assistance in the preparation of this book. I am deeply grateful for their collective contributions.

TABLE OF CONTENTS

INTRODUCTION

The concept of civility manages to be both one of timeless antiquity and modern relevance. As far back as the ancient Greeks, the warriors of Homer's *Iliad* were passionately focused on their ability to live up to the standards of their society by avoiding *ate*—a word often translated as sin, but more accurately denoting a failure to fulfill one's moral and social role. Jesus's Beatitudes focused on behaviors and attitudes that made for a peaceful, harmonious society. The Tao teaches its followers to live peaceful lives that ensure harmonious relationships with nature, with individuals, and with the Cosmos. Cultures from the West, Mid-East and East all echo this refrain: in order to have a functioning human society, members have to share some basic sense of what behavior towards others is acceptable and what is not.

Fast forward thousands of years, and note that matters haven't changed. While conventions have changed along with living conditions and technology, calls for behaviors consistent with a baseline norm of civility still fill the air. Thus when President Obama repeated his appeals for civility at the National Prayer Breakfast back in February of 2010 and again at the Commencement Ceremonies for the University of Michigan in May 2010, he was simply following a long and storied tradition of human social behavior—the instance of a figurehead calling for enforcement and practice of the social norms for interaction. Civility has once again become part of the national conversation. Citizens, politicians, students, and scholars are all now opening a new dialogue on civility and what it entails in modern culture. The many voices don't seem to agree on all the details of civil conduct, but the fact that they're having the conversation in the first place is a start.

The foundation is set. Civility is an ancient topic with a modern interest. But the remaining question is how to keep laying the bricks on this foundation. Dialogue is good, but it is meaningless if its participants lack the tools to create a workable framework.

We hope this book will contribute to this work. The prevailing assumption is that the modern university offers the best and most effective forum for providing an education in civility. Students currently entering their college years have a high degree of awareness of problems in their world and feel obligated to contribute to solving them. In this sense, they intuit the idea of contributing to the establishment of their *civitas*—the community in which they live.

In the pages that follow, we try to provide practical steps necessary for changing this latent desire to form stable social norms into a workable framework for a college-aged student. The framework builds on a single value: civility is defined as living according to the Golden Rule, doing unto others as you would have them do unto you, with respect for individual differences.

The devil is in the details. Our approach is to present scenarios of four real-life students—drawn from collective experience, anecdotal evidence, and hard data—who encounter civility dilemmas in the many spheres of university life. They face *tough* questions. They want to do the right thing, but regularly applying civility values proves to be difficult. The important part, though, is that the students think about the choices they make and whether those choices are in line with civil conduct. That sort of education is what can contribute to building of a modern, inclusive *civitas*.

1

I know of no more encouraging fact than the unquestionable ability of man to elevate his life by a conscious endeavor.

—Thoreau

WHY CIVILITY?

Common civility is becoming a lost art. In our busy and complex lives, simple gestures of politeness, such as smiling or saying "thank you," have become uncommon occurrences. The new norm has been to expect some level of rudeness and disrespect in just about every facet of our lives. People drive recklessly and without regard to others on the road. Many engage in loud and obnoxious cell phone conversations in restaurants, on buses, or even in movie theaters. Others deliberately litter, dropping trash in the streets and public areas such as parks. Rude and unprofessional behavior is pervasive in almost every sector of business.

Beyond the common acts of incivility that people encounter almost every day, shocking uncivil conduct among performing artists, athletes, and the occasional member of Congress seems to capture the attention of both the media and the public. Indeed, we've reached a point where incivility isn't just unremarkable[1]—it's considered marketable and entertaining.

The growing culture of incivility represents more than a lack of good manners; it is a lack of consideration for other people. If left unchecked, this lack of respect can perpetuate more incivility and can lead to even more dangerous uncivil conduct. Consider, for example, the string of Columbine-style shootings that have occurred in high schools, colleges, and shopping malls over the last decade. While determining why this type of incivility occurs is beyond the scope of this book, it is telling that in almost every case the perpetrators were social outcasts—in many cases subject to incivility by others. One study found that 90 percent of Americans believe incivility increases opportunity for violence.[2] In another survey eight in ten respondents said lack of respect and courtesy is a serious national problem.[3]

Although there is little public support or empathy for uncivil behavior, little is being done to curb such conduct. In fact, in some instances people may actually benefit from uncivil behavior. Brash and outrageous conduct catches media headlines and is essentially free publicity. Some may use shocking conduct to attract personal attention or attempt to gain notoriety. Incivility may also produce unintended benefits, as U.S. Representative Joseph Wilson discovered. Wilson's famous "You lie!" outburst during the 2009 State of the Union address resulted in donations totaling more than $1 million from individuals opposed to health-care reform.[4]

Civility is not innate. It must be instilled. Thus, incorporating concepts of civility and decency in the educational system makes sense.

Answering why we need another book on civility is both easy and difficult. Works such as P. M. Forni's *Choosing Civility: The Twenty-five Rules of Considerate Conduct*[5] and Stephen Carter's *Civility: Manners, Morals, and the Etiquette of Democracy*[6] do a great job of tackling the question of civility head-on, explaining what it is, why we need it, and what steps people can take to lead more civil and socially productive lives. In a sense, if everyone were to review the literature already out there and follow each author's reasoning and suggestions, we very well might be on our merry way to a utopian civil society.

Unfortunately, that hasn't panned out. Incivility remains a serious problem, not just because it is manifest in a lack of politeness or courtesy, but because it is the root of much more poignant problems in modern society, a lack of regard for others' rights, opinions, backgrounds, and beliefs. This disregard for others is the core problem for much of the violence, apathy, and remoteness in our culture, especially for young people. Expecting a person to take on a "heal thyself" approach to addressing incivility is too optimistic to have a profound effect on civility.

Instead, this book addresses some ways that students at modern American colleges encounter civility issues on campus. The complex interactions between students, their professors, and the community can create interesting challenges and conflicts. Sometimes there is no apparent right or wrong approach to avoiding the inherent tensions that exist when students transition to college life. However, when complicated relational issues are viewed through the lens of civility, students at least have a starting point to respond to the diverse array of problems they are likely to come across on campus.

WHAT IS CIVILITY?

So what does civility mean? *Civility* has been defined as "the state of being civilized" or "civil conduct."[7] In turn, being *civil* means "living in or exhibiting a condition of social advancement marked by organization and stability of community life or government: not uncivilized or primitive." These definitions are not much help in seeing how this term has much meaning for everyday life.

Forni encountered similar definitional problems, but decided to wrestle them into something useful. From polling his students at Johns Hopkins University, where he taught Italian literature, he developed four basic principles about civility: "(1) Civility is complex; (2) Civility is good; (3) Whatever civility might be, it has to do with courtesy, politeness, and good manners; and (4) Civility belongs in the realm of ethics."[8] From these principles, Forni concluded:

> Civility is a form of goodness; it is gracious goodness. But it is not just an attitude of benevolent and thoughtful relating to other individuals; it also entails an active interest in the well-being of our communities and even a concern for the health of the planet on which we live.[9]

Forni concedes his definition of civility is broad and inclusive, and the inclusive definition is just fine for his purposes, as his intention in *Choosing Civility* is to present twenty-five basic rules for the reader to follow in order to lead a life of civility. Instead of bogging down in the difficulties of finding a standard definition of the word, he offers more of a set of illustrations, painting what civil conduct *looks like* in various parts of life by instructing his readers how to engage in appropriate conduct in different situations.

In this, Forni is in good company. One of the most famous American descriptions of civility took a similar approach in describing the notion through specific rules of conduct. At the age of sixteen, George Washington copied *110 Rules of Civility & Decent Behavior in Company and Conversation*, apparently as part of an exercise in penmanship. Although Washington was only reciting these rules and not developing them, they are frequently associated with him. His legendary appropriate and polite conduct served him just about as well as his sense of duty and honor in becoming the country's greatest leader during its tumultuous early years.

In the end, this illustrative approach to defining civility is practical and helpful for everyday life, but it is simply too broad. Civility deserves a more focused definition that can serve us throughout this book. One place to start looking is the etymology of the word itself. The modern English word *civility* comes from the Latin word *civitas*, meaning "city," in the sense of civic community.[10] So in some sense, civility incorporates a notion that includes a personal responsibility to a community. This sense of civility might manifest in an individual's choice to contribute to the community through volunteer organizations, civic institutions, or even government. All of these behaviors demonstrate a concern not only for oneself, but also for the community in which one lives.

The other analytical foundation for the definition comes from a basic religious concept that is ancient and timeless: the Golden Rule. According to the Golden Rule, "You shall love your neighbor as yourself."[11] In other words, as long as people act with general regard for their neighbors and treat them with the same degree of respect and care that they would wish to be treated, they have fulfilled the requirement of the Golden Rule. By combining this principle with the idea that, by virtue of its own etymological history, civility carries with it the same obligation to a civic community writ large, we have a concrete notion of civility that can inform the rest of our discussion. Hence, civility is a combination of considerate conduct toward others embodied in the Golden Rule and a notion of civic duty and responsibility to the community.

So what does civility look like in practice? This is perhaps the easier question to answer. Civility usually is demonstrated through manners, courtesy, politeness, and a general awareness of the rights, wishes, concerns, and feelings of others. Showing deference to others, particularly those in authority, is another example of civil conduct. Civility can also be seen when a person is willing to embrace diversity and respect individuals with differing backgrounds, values, and beliefs. Making a point to listen to others and respond to the actual meanings they are trying to communicate—whether or not they are expressly articulated in words—is another example of civility.[12] Being mindful of the sensitivities of those with whom you speak and adjusting your own speech and conduct accordingly also demonstrates civility.[13] In this sense, civility is simply a form of personal conduct that shows respect and appreciation for others.

However, civility is more than just manners, politeness, and respect. The *civitas* side of civility calls for an individual to give of oneself to strengthen the community, usually at the sacrifice of one's own wishes and desires. In this sense, serving with a volunteer organization for the purpose of aiding others in the community is a form of civility. Likewise, running for public office—assuming that there are no ulterior selfish motives involved—also is a display of civility. We can think of it this way: while manners focus on the exchanges between and among individuals, civility also includes the exchange between an individual and the community. In fact, good manners and polite interactions with others foster a sense of community that strengthens the community as a whole.

Notice that until now our entire discussion has been on the positive side of civility. It might have been easier to take the opposite approach and begin with a definition of *incivility* first. *Incivility* has its own circular definition in the dictionary: "The quality or state of being uncivil: ill-bred behavior."[14] For the purposes of this book, incivility is defined as any self-centered behavior that is impolite or boorish or shows a disregard for rights and concerns for others. Incivility violates the Golden Rule by showing contempt for others in a way that the actor would presumably not want to be treated.

Similarly, more threatening behavior—using force for intimidation or disrupting public events with rowdy protests or vulgar behavior—is uncivil because it elevates the wants of one group (usually the minority) over the wants and needs of the entire community. Even behavior at the extreme of the scale—actions such as assault and murder—falls into the category of incivility because the same selfish motivations serve as the animating force. In this sense, even suicide can be deemed uncivil behavior because it shows a manifest disregard for the concerns of loved ones and the community's interest in preserving life.

WHY FOCUS ON THE COLLEGE CAMPUS?

Right now, there is a crisis of incivility on the American college campus. Notions of politeness, courtesy, and respect are increasingly yielding to a new wave of cultural influences that steer students out of the realm of genuine concern for others and into a pattern of intense self-absorption that undermines any civil society. Without a thoughtful and competent response, it's quite possible that civility as a notion and virtue won't endure much longer.

It might be easy to pass over the people vocalizing concerns of declining civil values as simply expressing a vague nostalgia for the "good old days" or dismay at changes in society that have nothing to do with actual civility. In some ways, this skepticism is warranted: researchers have repeatedly shown that older generations tend to view their successors as inferior in morality and personal virtues, often without cause.[15] And even if the current generation of college students exhibits more narcissism or inconsiderate behavior, this generation also is walking proof of *some* progress in the realm of civility. Today's college students represent a wide range of races, backgrounds, and ethnicities; just half a century ago, colleges tended to be populated by a homogenous group of white students to the exclusion of all others. At the very least, it's more consistent with the Golden Rule to have opened up the path to higher education to those of all colors.

But even so, the American campus exhibits signs of a generation that has either forgotten how to act civilly or never learned in the first place. Fans at sporting events have directed profane chants directly to the other team's individual players, even taunting them with reminders of past horrific conduct.[16] Out-of-control student conduct forced one large university to create a Task Force on Preventing Celebratory Riots just to respond to a series of violent outbursts over a decade that caused several injuries and thousands of dollars of property damage.[17] By most accounts, rape and sexual assault on college campuses are at an all-time high.[18] The brutal shooting rampage at Virginia Polytechnic Institute and State University on April 16, 2007, which left 33 people dead, served as a shocking reminder that some college students have reached the level of so disregarding the rights and interests of others that they are ready to take the lives of others as well as their own.[19]

Many college administrators seem to be uncertain about how to respond to the incivility crisis. Their hesitation is certainly understandable; the college's role as an institution has become progressively murky. Nearly four hundred years ago, when the colonial government of Massachusetts founded Harvard University, the universal understanding of higher education was that it was meant to develop male students' intellectual curiosity and moral fiber.[20] Most colleges were sponsored by the church, which had a vested interest in developing the spiritual health of its pool of future clergy. Administrators took a strict, paternal approach in correcting the students' moral failings and promoting civil, socially beneficial conduct.[21] In effect, colleges were seen to stand in the place of the family in providing students with moral instruction and civic lessons so that they could become contributing members of society. This notion was reflected in the term used to describe the university's role, *in loco parentis*, a Latin term literally meaning "in the place of a parent."[22] This remained the standard system with little change until the American Civil War in the middle of the nineteenth century.

The paternalistic view of education has deep roots. Going all the way back to the ancient Greek civilization, educators assumed two objectives: "(1) forming moral character and (2) enabling [students] to become members of a community."[23] Aristotle went so far as to describe education solely in terms of moral instruction: its goal was to "to make [men] good and disposed to do what is noble."[24] So when Noah Webster observed, "Education...forms the moral characters of men, and morals are the basis of government,"[25] he was working with a rich Western educational tradition in which teachers sought to instill morality and virtue—in a word, civility—into the character of their students.

Immediately after the Civil War, however, colleges across the country experienced a radical change in their organizational philosophy. The shift began with the founding of Johns Hopkins University in 1876. Johns Hopkins was the first American college to successfully reject the English system paradigm of fostering a family-like atmosphere of moral development and the pursuit of knowledge and replace it with the German system of higher education, which focused on individualized research and personal development.[26] Colleges across the nation quickly followed suit and permanently changed to the new German model.[27]

The modern state of American education can be seen as one of uneasy, temporary stasis. While large colleges have almost universally made an explicit shift away from the traditional *in loco parentis* model of developing their students' character, primary and secondary schools have also latched on to elements of the more individualistic German model. Since 1969, the courts have recognized a First Amendment right of expression for minor students in public schools.[28] As appealing as it is for students to have a right to free speech, it sometimes stands in direct contradiction to the valid interests of public educators who seek to instill a sense of moral virtue and civility in their students. Rules seeking to promote these virtues now have to pass constitutional review.[29]

So today's college administrators face a very daunting task. Not only are their own institutions poorly equipped as a result of the shift to the German model to instill students with the moral education that college once provided, but they also are accepting students who have long been taught with hardly any reference to this role for educators. As a result, modern university administrators are stuck with the same responsibilities and concerns for fostering the growth of a virtuous and socially conscious student body without the accompanying tools for enforcing rules making them into such a group. In fact, some administrators might validly question whether the new higher education model leaves any role for such schooling in the first place.

Further complicating matters, the students themselves probably are confused about the proper role of their university teachers and administrators in teaching character development and civility. When students are essentially given the impression that moral education isn't even a proper role for secondary teachers, they'll certainly be confused—and perhaps irritated—by any heavy-handed attempts to teach civility by college administrators after being told repeatedly by the media and parents that they're independent adults in society.

A necessary part of prescribing actions that college administrators and faculty should take to nurture civility in their students, then, is defining the modern role of administrators in the first place. Upon closer inspection, there is still room for a moral education, even in the modern model of institutions for higher learning; it will just have to be adapted to today's students. Administrators have an opportunity to make the most out of this role and move to the front line in promoting a culture of civility on the American college campus.

WHO ARE THE STUDENTS NOW ENTERING COLLEGE?

The current generation of college students shares a defined system of values, habits, beliefs, and expectations that would—in any other time in history—quickly demand a name and a categorization by a sociologist. But this generation manages to also show a strong sense of diversity in beliefs and values, and a strong aversion to labeling that has enabled it to avoid a single name thus far. It is variously called Generation Y,[30] Generation Next,[31] the Millennials,[32] the Echo Boomers,[33] the MTV Generation,[34] the Net Generation, and the Boomerang Generation. The very difficulty in finding the appropriate term serves as a cautionary note to efforts to overgeneralize the traits and values of its members. Just as sociologists William Strauss and Neil Howe chose to do in their important work *The History of America's Future, 1584 to 2069*, we'll tentatively refer to this generation as "Millennials"— using a name that they chose for themselves as a means of distinguishing themselves from their predecessors, Generation X.[35]

There is some foundational irony to the idea of teaching Millennials the virtue of how to respectfully interact with others. One of the few things about which most scholars seem to agree is that the generation has set new records for its capacity to communicate and connect with one another. Millennials are the first generation to experience the phenomenon of online social networks (and the first to have Internet access during their developmental years) and the first to carry portable forms of immediate communication—from pagers in the early 1990s to modern handheld wireless devices, capable of sending emails and text messages from almost anywhere in the world. American teenagers send and receive, on average, 2,899 text messages each month and make or receive 191 phone calls on their cell phones.[36] Millennials seem to have taken the idea of creating social networks and friends to a new, digital level, making past conventions governing civility in these types of relationships somewhat dated.

The news isn't all bad when it comes to Millenials' values and sense of community obligations. Two different comprehensive surveys—the University of California at Los Angeles's survey The American Freshman National Norms for Fall 2008[37] and the Pew Research Center's How Young People View Their Lives, Futures and Politics: A Portrait of "Generation Next"[38]—indicate that Millennials are more dedicated to helping others and performing social service than recent generations. The same findings are repeated in the works by scholars examining the Millennial generation.[39]

With these virtues, there are also clear signs of problems with civility in the Millennials. This young generation tends to exhibit signs of self-absorption, indicating a lack of awareness for the needs and concerns of others. One effect of this lack of general civility is that Millennials have had trouble adjusting to workplaces where they do not receive special attention or recognition for performing tasks for superiors who are presumably of older generations.[40] Millennials also have displayed an affinity for decidedly uncivil music, films, and art, with themes of violence, casual sex, and general self-absorption pervading each medium.

Broad descriptions of a generation encompassing more than two million young adults are useful only to a point. It is much more beneficial to move to more concrete depictions. The next chapter introduces four fictional members of the Millennial generation—Antonio, Lindsey, Sonam, and Jacob—who are all beginning school at some nameless large American university. Each brings a unique set of interests, values, concerns, and experiences. But these are useful values, experiences, and interests to study because they're based on real data and stories about the Millennial generation. Observing the civically tricky situations that the students encounter and watching how they respond to them capture how large segments of the current college population view the world. For the remainder of the book, we'll follow these four to show what can be done to foster the spirit of civility on the American college campus.

2

Don't discount the power of your words. The thought that they might cause unnecessary hurt or discomfort should inform every conversation.

—P. M. Forni

CIVILITY AND THE GREEK SYSTEM

It might seem odd to begin a discussion of civility on the college campus by looking at fraternities and sororities. After all, Greeks comprise a minority of students on most college campuses—sometimes, a very small minority.[1] However, the reality is that on campuses that have Greek organizations, the Greek system exerts a profound effect on the entire campus culture.

Various stereotypes are associated with fraternities and sororities. Many people think that Greek organizations are synonymous with hazing, wild parties, and alcohol and drug abuse. Others view Greek organizations as elitist social clubs for spoiled rich kids that discriminate against minorities, gays, and overweight individuals.

Although these stereotypes may fit some fraternities and sororities, they are not representative of all. In addition to creating friendships and networks of professional and personal support, many fraternities and sororities make large positive contributions to the university community and the world at large. Greek organizations encourage their members to participate in campus activities and other school-related organizations in a way reflecting the notion of *civitas* of the ancients—an obligation to serve one's community.[2]

For example, undergraduate Greek students annually volunteer approximately 850,000 hours and raise about $7 million for charities. As alumni, Greeks are more involved in their communities and give more generously than non-Greek alums.[3] The influence of the Greek system doesn't end with those enrolled in school—considering that 76 percent of U.S. senators, 85 percent of Fortune 500 executives, and 85 percent of U.S. Supreme Court justices since 1910 could claim membership in a Greek organization.[4]

The valuable societal contributions made by Greek students and alumni are significant and should not be marginalized. Nonetheless, Greek organizations have also significantly contributed to the culture of incivility that is pervasive at many colleges and universities.

Research has demonstrated that fraternities and sororities are among the key groups that foster the culture of drinking on campus.[5] According to the Harvard School of Public Health's College Alcohol Study, 75 percent of fraternity members engage in heavy drinking, compared to 49 percent of other male students.[6] Likewise, 62 percent of sorority members engaged in heavy drinking, compared with 41 percent of other female students.[7] Since Greek students drink more than others, they also suffer from more alcohol-related problems than their peers, such as poor academic performance, fights, serious injuries, and sexual assault.[8]

Understanding the Greek system is important to understanding university dynamics—and civility on campus—because Greek organizations at many schools control the social activities and campus governments.[9] Candidates for elected positions ranging from Miss Homecoming to Student Government Association president usually rely on the name association and manpower afforded by membership in their fraternity or sorority—and often their success is entirely dependent on the persuasive appeal of their Greek friends. The data suggest that membership in a large enough Greek organization may by itself be almost enough to get someone elected—when only about 20 percent of the student population votes in a student government election, a few hundred votes may be enough to win.[10]

This chapter will provide a historical overview of Greek organizations, describe the membership process, and then examine several Greek life trends that promote incivility through the experiences of the four freshman students in our extended hypothetical.

A HISTORY OF THE GREEK SYSTEM

The Greek organizations first developed on American university campuses in the late eighteenth century. For the most part, they were formed as intellectual organizations that focused on providing a forum for serious discussions and camaraderie among members. From the beginning of the nineteenth century to the 1870s, the Greek fraternities—which were almost exclusively male and white—grew more into a social network that mirrored secret societies.[11] Universities generally regarded the fraternities as "valuable adjuncts of student life and, instead of opposing them, most institutions decided that they might be put to work helping run the school, keeping recalcitrant students in line, acting as convenient units of discipline in college life."[12]

As the popularity of the fraternities grew, so did demands for similar groups open to women and minorities. In the late nineteenth and early twentieth centuries, sororities were established for white women as a forum for discussing topics such as "literature, poetry, and morality."[13] Around the turn of the twentieth century, fraternities for African-American men also developed to offer opportunities in networking and intellectual development, and sororities for African-American women followed.[14]

While these forerunners established the roots for the modern Greek system, the current structure developed in the postwar boom of the 1940s and 1950s. As veterans flocked to colleges in record numbers, the ranks of Greek organizations swelled proportionately.[15] Over time, the Greek organizations became the *de facto* controller of many facets of campus life and achieved a dominant role on college campuses.

As of the year 2000, the Center for the Study of the College Fraternity at Indiana University reported that 324 educational institutions recognize Greek organizations. These fraternities and sororities claimed 242,332 active members and 86,450 pledges.[16] Although the numbers are hard to nail down with any degree of specificity, the general trend seems to be that there are fewer Greeks on campus than there were in the past. The Center's 2000 study reported that Greeks comprised an average of 17.5 percent of the student body at the reporting schools and a median of 12 percent of students.

BECOMING GREEK

At many institutions Greek organizations hold the special distinction of being the first major example of campus culture that entering freshmen encounter. Rush week, the recruitment period for sororities and fraternities, usually occurs in the fall semester, before classes or even athletics really start. During rush week, new students interested in joining or pledging a fraternity or sorority have an opportunity to evaluate the various Greek organizations on campus. This evaluation process typically occurs through a series of formal and informal events and parties hosted by each Greek organization on campus. While these events are designed to give candidates an opportunity to learn about the organizations, they also give the organizations an opportunity to evaluate potential members.

Fraternities and sororities are highly selective and base membership decisions on an array of criteria that may range from academic achievement to personal appearance. Ultimately, during rush week, the main objective of fraternities and sororities is to pledge quality members—that is, members who share their values, but also members who will be able to attract other recruits in the future. Maintaining a certain image may be equally important to some Greek organizations as more substantive criteria. For example, one sorority used "boob ranking" to determine membership.[17]

When a fraternity or sorority selects a candidate for membership, it offers the student a bid or an official invitation to become a member. During rush week, some students may receive bids from multiple Greek organizations while others may receive none. Students who accept bids pledge to become a new member of the organization, although they are not full members until they successfully complete a pledge period and initiation.

Depending on the organization, the pledge period varies from a few weeks to more than a year. It is designed to test the loyalty and commitment of each student pledging and determine whether he or she is worthy of membership. Pledges have heavy demands placed on their time by their fraternity or sorority. They may be required to wear a pledge pin; learn about the organization, its history and values; and attend meetings and social events with current members. Pledges may also be required to clean the organization's house after parties or serve as designated drivers for other members. Not all who pledge will become members. Those who successfully complete the pledge period usually undergo some form of initiation.

COMPULSIVE CONFORMITY

One of the ways Greek life may demonstrate incivility is by demanding that members conform to strict character molds. Greek organizations may also exhibit a very stubborn reluctance to accept others. Even though the mission statements of many Greek organizations expressly include provisions articulating a commitment to diversity and inclusion, some tend to brush aside unique and meaningful characteristics, integrate members into a homogenous whole, and reject prospects who can't fit the image the organization is attempting to project.

Lindsey

The general conversational buzz from graduation at Cooke County High School had scarcely died away before most of the talk had shifted to a new direction: Sorority Rush, only two short months away. Lindsey got uncharacteristically caught up in it, too, which can only be expected when surrounded by the chatter every day. Like forty other classmates, she was headed to the nearby university and completely thrilled by the idea of venturing away from home for the first time. Joining a sorority—even with its known demands on time, energy, and willpower—seemed to be an excellent way to branch out on this freedom and meet new people.

The summer flew by, and Lindsey soon found herself moving into an on-campus dorm on the first Sunday in August, with the first rush week event scheduled for the next morning at Sigma. She arrived a few minutes early with a high school friend and found a line of other girls in summer dresses and strappy heels already spilling out the door. Once inside, they were both greeted by a very caffeinated, very enthusiastic sister who assured them repeatedly how happy she was to see them there. Handed a napkin and a plastic cup, they were pointed to a punch bowl on a table near the front door.

"So far, so good," whispered Lindsey, keeping a pleasant—but not quite exuberant—smile on her face. Her friend Laura appeared engrossed by the napkins they had been handed. "What on earth are you looking at?"

Laura's tight smile barely concealed some real agitation. "I knew it. God, I hoped it was just a story, but I knew it had to be true," she whispered hurriedly. "The napkins, Linz—see how they're handing them out in random colors, purple and yellow?" Lindsey nodded but without much concern. There were plenty of oddities in college already to forgive arbitrary napkin bestowal. "It's a sign," continued Laura. "Melissa told me all about it. The cute girls get one color, and the ugly ones get a different one. It's the sorority's way of getting rid of prospects right away to avoid wasting time with bad rushers."

Lindsey looked down at her purple napkin. Her stomach tightened a bit. It took a desperate effort to avoid spending the rest of the time at the Sigmas' house figuring out what kind of token she held.

By the end of the day, Lindsey had visited twelve sororities and walked away convinced that Ralph Lauren did not make clothes to fit anyone over a size four. She had had eighty-seven conversations—she counted—with sisters of all the sororities, who were inevitably enthusiastic, warm-mannered, stylishly dressed, and bone thin. All talked about the importance of having people to back you up when you're struggling with tough classes at school. Less emphasized—but clearly intended to be heard—were the claims of invitations to only the best parties with the coolest fraternities. And while no one came out and said it, there was an undertone that resonated throughout the day: the sororities were going to be picky about who got in. Not everyone was pretty, connected, smart, and charming enough to belong.

Selectivity

Lindsey's experience during Sorority Rush seemed to underscore the tendencies of some Greek organizations to disregard diversity. According to Lindsey, almost every sorority sister was "inevitably enthusiastic, warm-mannered, stylishly dressed, and bone thin." While it is uncertain whether the "purple napkin" was some type of signal to the sorority, Lindsey immediately felt her nerves start to kick in. Was she pretty enough? Did she make the right impression? What would happen if she was rejected?

Fraternities and sororities are highly selective, which may create inherent diversity challenges. Nevertheless, when decisions are made on such arbitrary criteria as appearance, image, and where a person shops for clothes, it is easy to see how fraternities and sororities can perpetuate uniformity. But what may be even more detrimental is the skewed sense of community that is created among members. Acceptance is based on conformity, not diversity.

The *New York Times* reported that the national leadership of a sorority at one university had intervened when the chapter's membership had fallen drastically. After a campus visit, the leadership determined that twenty-three of the thirty-five members lacked sufficient commitment to recruitment, and they were asked to assume alumnae status and leave the sorority house. The members asked to leave included all the overweight members and ethnic minorities and the editor of the student newspaper. The remaining women were, according to the article, "slender and popular with fraternity men." The move provoked an intense reaction on campus. Six of the remaining twelve members withdrew from the sorority, and parents, alumni, and faculty members voiced their strong opposition. The university president reprimanded the sorority for its action.[18] The divergence between the national leadership and chapter membership brings up an interesting question: Is there room for a fraternity or sorority chapter that intentionally recruits diverse membership?

PRESSURES OF PLEDGING

Once a student accepts a bid and pledges to a fraternity or sorority, he or she must begin the process of demonstrating loyalty to the organization before becoming a full member. This process can be very demanding and sometimes just plain brutal. Pledges may be required to be at the whim and call of the other members. Failure to adequately comply with the sometimes outrageous requests of the brothers or sisters of the fraternity or sorority could cost the pledge membership. There is immense pressure to make a good impression, even if it means participating in activities that may go against the student's sense of right and wrong.

Jacob

Unlike most of his friends, Jacob wasn't in any hurry at all to start college in the fall. He had enjoyed high school, had become close friends with his classmates for more than eight years, and didn't see college as the golden ticket to personal freedom—his parents were generally pretty cool with that kind of stuff. Even though the university was across town from his house, school seemed like an unnecessarily dramatic transition away from the comfortable life he had known.

Nonetheless, August came despite Jacob's doubts, and he soon found himself moving into a new life. He had decided to live on campus despite its proximity to his parents' house in a good-faith effort to get the real college experience. But this was about as far as he was willing to go. Other traditional social parts of school—fraternities, sports, student government groups—just weren't in the cards for him, at least not yet.

Jacob didn't have any hang-ups about using the existing social systems for all they were worth, however. His first week on campus, he saw—along with everyone else—the flyers from the Beta house advertising a band party starting at 11:00 Friday night. All it took was one invitation from a high school classmate who had pledged Beta, and he was all for it.

"Tight party, huh?" Adam asked as he and Jacob wove through the crowd toward the back of the frat house. Jacob thought about speaking his concurrence, but the noise from the band foreclosed the opportunity, and he simply nodded. It was pretty impressive—a popular local country/rock group was jamming in front of a crowd of college students, pretty girls sporting denim and heels, and guys all adorned in fashionable fall hues offered by Polo and La Coste. A garbage can with a plastic liner and hunch punch sat inconspicuously in a corner, ready to be whisked away at the first sign of trouble.

The only blip so far had been relatively minor. One of the older frat brothers had decided he didn't really care for one pledge's girlfriend. He decided to express himself with a candor provoked by alcohol and lack of inhibitions.

"Listen, Waller, I'm tired of you here. And your pig of a girlfriend has to go. She's done nothing but guzzle our stuff without bringing a single hot chick along with her. Just unacceptable, man… unless you're getting some sort of bonus in hitting that, she ain't worth it."

These thoughts had never occurred to Waller. He froze. His girlfriend turned with red eyes moistened and moved by the punch and the words.

"You need to go home. Come on, I'll take you," Waller managed to spit out softly. He turned to the brother. "Sorry about that—I'll be back soon."

"Yeah, and bring us some smokes."

The incident passed without significant notice. The girl's' friends first stood stiffly with indignation, but were forced to relax as the frat brothers continued making jokes at the excluded one's expense. The party continued.

That is, it continued until the next disturbance. Matthew, a young pledge who was generally well liked, finally had all the alcohol he could take in the evening and collapsed onto a couch in the corner, shoes still on. Jacob saw this coming and quickly felt sorry for him, knowing what was next. Falling out with boots on in a frat party is a cardinal sin. It makes you fair game for any level of abuse the other partygoers feel like inflicting. Using sharpies, stripping off clothing—you name it, and it can happen.

And it did. It was pretty mild stuff—just some impromptu Sharpie tattoos and stripping the pledge down to his boxers. But as Jacob watched, he realized that the tattoo artists had slowly abandoned their work and backed off as a more sober frat member dashed to find the fraternity president. They had noticed that Matthew's breathing had grown more and more shallow and that he hadn't responded to even the most intrusive pokes of their abuse.

Gaining Acceptance

In the heat of the moment, pledges may go along with the pressure, even if they have serious reservations. The quirky requirements placed on pledges may seem more like harmless pranks rather than offensive or potentially hazardous behavior.[19] Nevertheless, the demeaning requirements sometimes placed on pledges, along with the pressure to comply with such requirements to gain acceptance, demonstrate incivility toward the students pledging as well as others.

Jacob witnessed the brazen disrespect that can exist between fraternity members and pledges at his first frat party. At the party, one pledge was berated for having a "pig of a girlfriend" who did not bring "a single hot chick." It was interesting that the pledge did not attempt to defend his girlfriend, but went along with the offensive behavior. The fraternity's behavior could simply be chalked up to juvenile pranks. However, the implications of this single event could have far-reaching effects, not just to the ejected girl, but to everyone present. For instance, the partygoers learned that acceptance was based on superficial criteria, such as appearance and associations. This notion of community can be toxic to the campus community because it elevates conformity over individuality at the expense of individuals who do not fit the mold.

The experience of pledging often blends into another ubiquitous part of Greek life: alcohol. Fraternities and sororities are notorious for their part in fostering the college practice of binge drinking—along with its accompanying hazards. Pledges are often expected to purchase and consume alcohol despite being under legal drinking age. But they are by no means the only ones who get intoxicated at Greek social events. Alcohol is often available to everyone who comes to the parties, leading to heavy drinking by thousands of students each weekend.

Jacob saw a pledge pass out drunk during the party. While the fraternity regarded this as an opportune time for pranks, the atmosphere of the party changed quickly when the pledge became unresponsive. What may appear to be harmless fun can have devastating consequences.

HAZING

Following the pledge period, the initiation includes secret traditions and rituals that vary by organization. New members are sworn to keep the organization's traditions and rituals secret. While the initiation may be as innocuous as using secret mottos, handshakes, and passwords, in some organizations the initiations may go farther. An initiation that humiliates, degrades, abuses, or endangers an individual, regardless of the person's willingness to participate, is considered hazing.[20] Hazing typically involves coercing alcohol consumption, but may also include requiring pledges to endure sleep deprivation, undergo physical and verbal abuse, engage in humiliating sex acts, or participate in strenuous physical activity.[21] Some students might view hazing as harmless pranks, but the practice often results in serious injuries and sometimes death. Since 1970, there has been at least one hazing-related death on a college campus each year.[22]

Antonio

"So are you gonna do it?"

Antonio and David were cycling out reps on the bench, and the question seemed to come out of nowhere. Antonio looked up in mild surprise at his friend. Not that the topic was in question or the question ambiguous, but he still wanted to make sure.

"Do what?"

"Rush, man. Don't be stupid. It starts next week."

Yeah, I know. The point itself was stupid, given the amount of thought that rush week had already gotten from both young men. February 1— start of spring baseball practices—was almost an entire six months away, and more pressing issues had replaced the thoughts of scholarships and major league drafts that had totally consumed the minds of both of them. The now, the immediate, demanded that Antonio make some decisions.

"I dunno. Still thinking."

"Hell, you thought enough. You've probably already made your mind up, just don't want to say. I'm gonna rush."

That last sentence was meant to be provocative. Being able to hang out with David on a campus with more than twenty thousand strangers was a bit of a godsend, and missing his company for a week—possibly the rest of their time in college—was not a very promising option.

But David probably was right. Antonio probably *had thought* enough. He had thought about a ton of things that probably never occurred to David. He thought about his name and the slightly browner tint of his skin and how that might impact his odds for getting in with the right frat. He thought about the stuff he'd have to deal with even if he got in the door— rumors were that the pledge captains at Alpha house were out for blood this year. He had also thought about the easy avenues that membership provided to the most obvious joys of college life—alcohol, women, and acceptance. He thought about how his future teammates would look at him if he were one of the few scholarship baseball players not rushing.

But thinking, he finally decided, didn't solve anything. "Sure," he said. "Why not?"

Antonio got his answer a few weeks later. When the Alpha brothers had promised hell, they weren't kidding. One week into his pledgeship, and Antonio had already been forced to consume a can of chew (by eating it), a dozen eggs, food wiped and otherwise debauched by contact with all parts of the brothers' bodies, two fifths of vodka, and about a dozen beers. He was now balancing on his knees and chin, dressed in a girl's (too small) cheerleading outfit while the Alpha brothers and their invited guests—the sisters of Zeta—paraded around them, laughing and poking. The fact that the rest of his future baseball teammates were in the same position wasn't much comfort.

Harmless Prank Or Criminal Offense?

Hazing is illegal in most states, and in some states it is considered a felony. Despite the fact that hazing could be a criminal offense, the practice still occurs. Moreover, students affected by hazing rarely report the incidents. This may be partially due to the secret nature of the initiation process and the fact that nine out of ten students who have experienced hazing do not consider themselves to have been hazed.[23]

One tragic example of fraternity hazing gone wrong occurred at Chico State University in 2005. During an initiation, fraternity brothers ordered pledges to do calisthenics in raw sewage that had leaked on the basement floor of the fraternity's house and then interrogated and taunted them for hours.[24] While confined to the basement of the house, pledges were ordered to drink from a five-gallon jug of water that was filled repeatedly. Scribbled on the walls was the phrase, "In the basement, no one can hear you scream."[25] Pledges were forced to vomit and urinate on themselves as fans blew cold air on their wet bodies. During the ritual, one pledge collapsed and had a seizure. He died of water intoxication, which caused swelling of his brain and lungs. Four of the fraternity brothers responsible for the hazing were convicted of felony hazing and were sentenced to a year in jail.[26]

While hazing is most commonly associated with Greek organizations, it also occurs in other student groups, such as marching bands, ski clubs, church groups, and other social and academic clubs. In fact, more than half of the students who belong to campus organizations experienced hazing.[27] Every national fraternity and virtually every university with a Greek system prohibits hazing. Yet despite state laws and institutional policies prohibiting hazing, the practice occurs, often shrouded by secrecy and the guise of tradition.

So based on what we know, was Antonio hazed? Without a doubt, yes. Being coerced to consume large amounts of alcohol and to eat debauched food is classic hazing. Likewise, the humiliation he endured from his fraternity brothers, and their invited sorority guests, while he was dressed as a cheerleader could be considered a form of hazing.

ALTERNATIVES TO GREEK LIFE

Greek life is not for everyone. Yet very few social alternatives are available at some schools. Greek organizations may dominate campus culture by default. Fraternity and sorority houses are frequently located in prominent areas of the campus. The social events they host are popular with students and often provide students access to alcohol. The largest on-campus drinking venues are fraternity and sorority houses.[28]

When one considers the proximity of Greek houses on campus, along with the popular parties they host, it is easier to see how the organizations can control student life and campus culture.[29] Students who are looking for social opportunities outside the Greek system often feel frustrated by their lack of options.

Sonam

Heading into the final weeks of her last semester of high school, Sonam already was wishing the summer away and dreaming about college that fall. Sure, summer marked the end of classes, but it also brought the promise of two more months in the small town of Marion. Sonam thought she had little to look forward to over that time, with her expected rounds of babysitting and working as a hostess at the local restaurant. Making the occasional late night round with friends at Starbucks and hitting up a few concerts within a day's drive seemed to be the most promising options, but even they paled in comparison to the fall to come.

For Sonam, the promise of school away from home was the fulfillment of most of her hopes and dreams. Instead of continuing to waste away with a small group of friends, a big imagination, and little to exercise it on, she felt that college promised a fresh start filled with possibilities and people. For once, she thought, she wouldn't be a conspicuous outsider. Although seven years in town had erased any remnants of her parents' mild Indian accent in her speech, she still felt self-conscious in her high school, standing out in a sea of white faces and regional accents. *College won't be like this—it will be bigger.*

The summer passed more quickly than she expected, and before she knew what was happening, Sonam found herself waving good-bye to her parents as they pulled out of the dorm parking lot. Freedom had arrived, but it was of a daunting sort. Never one to shy away from a challenge, Sonam headed back into her dorm and struck up a conversation with the two girls who lived in the adjoining room.

Not surprisingly, the topic on their minds was rush week. The festivities began the next morning, and the two girls were excitedly discussing proprieties and expectations.

Sonam didn't respond right away. She knew, of course, that rush began the next day—it provided a great reason for her to get away from home a week sooner than otherwise would happen. But she hadn't decided yet whether to venture out into the thick of things. Rush week was a known time of high anxiety and nerves—maybe more than she needed to start off her new life. Even more troubling, the campus sororities hadn't exactly gone out of their way to kill off their reputations as WASP-y groups that probably wouldn't fall all over themselves to find a new member who didn't look identical to them. It sounded like more trouble than it was worth.

Nonetheless, Sonam played a good sport to her neighbors' earnest requests for her to go along, and she got up early the next morning to prepare and make it to Sigma at 9:00. All in all, it was a bit better than expected; the sisters seemed genuinely nice, and Sonam found several who had similar tastes in singer-songwriter music and granola rock.

But despite all this, Sonam had made up her mind by the time she returned to her room late that afternoon: rushing just wasn't for her. While she probably could find a sorority that wasn't too concerned about her name or skin color and provided some affable friends, it just seemed too cheap, too convenient... too much like small-town high school. Sonam had come to school to see the world, but the world she saw in the Greek system seemed to be pretty small.

Anxious to find something else to keep her occupied that week—organizing closets can only take so long—Sonam scanned the weekly university email to see what else was going on. She was taken aback by the paucity of university-sanctioned events before class started. She got the sense that the school had learned to leave rush week to the Greeks and wait until classes started to focus on the rest of the student body. There was, however, an open house sponsored by the international student group for the next evening. Figuring that she didn't have much choice, Sonam opted to check it out.

The open house was a disappointment. The students there were nice, but they had even less in common with Sonam than the sisters at rush. Most were foreign nationals who were still adjusting to life in the United States. Although she usually wasn't one to worry needlessly, Sonam began to feel a bit concerned. Nothing at the university seemed to cater to *her*—to what she liked, to what she felt, to what she did. Instead, the groups on campus appeared to pull students into a homogenous pile that trumped individualities.

Finding A Place To Fit In

The transition from the familiarities of high school to the uncertainties of college life can be overwhelming. Finding a place to fit in, especially at a large campus, is critically important. Making friends and social connections is a key component of a student's integration into the campus. Fraternities and sororities provide a convenient way to engage the campus community, but Greek life is not for everyone.

Sonam's reluctance to rush was based in large part on her concerns that she did not fit the stereotypical image of a sorority girl. Despite her hesitancy to rush, she decided to give it a try and was pleasantly surprised that some sororities were not "too concerned about her name or skin color." Nevertheless, Sonam decided against joining a sorority.

Upon making her decision, she quickly learned that her university just did not have many other social options available to students during the first few weeks on campus. What was more frustrating for Sonam was that the campus community seemed to pull students into homogenous groups with very minimal integration.

3

A teacher learns flexibility through practice, becoming more adept at anticipating and avoiding incivility.

—Steven Richardson

CIVILITY IN THE CLASSROOM

The core civility issues lie at the heart of the university itself: the classroom. Most students in America have regular interactions in a campus classroom and at campus events, unlike aspects such as Greek life and athletics, which represent only a fraction of all college and graduate students.[1] Whether these interactions involve discussions in and out of class between students and professors, between students assigned to work together on a project, or even between friends who happen to take the same class together, they all touch on important issues of civility.

Often issues with civility in the classroom are more commonly recognized by more specific names: cheating, plagiarism, and academic integrity. School officials often address these topics in terms of specific policies such as honor codes and with remedies that are often nothing more than a small bandage for a much bigger problem. Issues involving classroom civility must be seen in a larger context that includes basic relational issues and concepts of respect and tolerance for the ideas and values of others.

The knee-jerk reaction to an effort to address issues of civility in the classroom might be to view the students as the exclusive source of uncivil comments and behaviors. While it's probably true that most issues of civility in the classroom involve students and their attitudes and behaviors toward their professors and others, the background issues leading to uncivil situations come from many systemic civility deficiencies of the university. In this chapter, we'll try to provide a comprehensive look at the issues involving civility in the classroom, using our same four characters as before.

PRESSURE TO CHEAT

The most recent research from the Center for Academic Integrity (CAI) shows that 70 percent of college students on surveyed campuses admitted to cheating.[2] Nearly one-quarter of students admitted to cheating on tests, and half admitted to cheating on written assignments. Other forms of cheating, such as plagiarism and improper student collaboration, were also on the rise.[3]

Students are frequently seduced into cheating in an attempt to get ahead, keep up, or just save time. Despite the implementation of honor codes and tough sanctions and attempts by schools to promote academic integrity, students encounter intense pressures to succumb to cheating, as Antonio learned firsthand.

Antonio

"Mr. Juarez, are you still with us?"

Antonio jolted, thrusting his back into the chair. "Yes," he said in a firm, but slightly embarrassed voice. The telltale trailing lines going from his last line of notes on how the demand curve shifts when…. (with gibberish below the line) showed him that despite his best efforts, he had drifted off.

"Good," Professor Austin replied, showing he was amused, but not angry. "I was asking about finding the new equilibrium price, and you looked like you were dying to answer."

Antonio walked to the whiteboard and made the crooked lines that seem to come naturally to econ types trying to draw a graph. This stuff was pretty familiar to him—so far, nothing far removed from high school material. He managed a reply that was close enough to correct to acquit him of any further embarrassment.

God, I have to get some sleep, he thought. College so far had proved to be a disorienting array of opportunities and obligations—neither of which left much time for sleep. He had been out until the early morning twice this week already on pledge duties, and the English project he had been putting off for a while remained a daunting sleep stealer for tonight. Despite this exhausting regimen, he managed to prop his eyelids open for the last five minutes of class.

It wasn't long before he had some help. At the end of the period, Professor Austin handed back their graded midterms—"So you won't stress over them the whole time," they were told. Antonio unfolded his to find a big, ugly 67 staring him in the face. That wasn't good—in fact, it was shockingly bad. It was a subject he knew at least something about, and a 67 was way below the B average he kept in high school.

His mind immediately went into overdrive. *What exactly went wrong? I mean, I did study for it last Tuesday night. Well, okay, studied with Keri and David for about two hours… which we mostly spent making fun of some of the girls in Keri's sorority. But still, I've kept up in class—this shouldn't be like this.*

In reality, as much as Antonio hated to see that score with his name attached to it, the consequences weren't anything dire. His scholarship and eligibility status were safe as long as he passed—and with a midterm comprising only 25 percent of his total grade and plenty of projects, homework, and papers to make up the bulk of it, he had plenty of time to recover. Still, he'd rather not stay on the frat's dog list—reserved for pledges with GPAs under 2.8—and be forced to keep regular study hours in the library for another semester.

"So, how was it? Bitch of a test, huh?"

Antonio turned and saw Ryan, a sophomore who was in his fraternity. "Yeah, it was."

"Hey, look—you know the trick to this, right? Austin's too damn lazy to actually come up with new tests every year. We've got a box full of his old ones back at the house. This one was straight out of fall 2005, with only the order moved around."

Antonio actually didn't know the trick. This was news to him—frustrating and great news, all at once. "Man—didn't know that. I'll definitely need to go look before the final. Does he know about it?"

Ryan laughed. "What do you think? Look, all of the sororities and even the Honors dorm have the same system for almost any professor in the school. So it's nothing to worry about. Tell you what—tonight let's both do the homework and I'll show you where the treasure box is."

Antonio paused. The idea of old tests floating around seemed a bit odd, maybe even unfair, but it was a long way from *cheating*. Plus, if everyone else on the curve was looking at them, he'd be stupid not to. But the homework offer wasn't as innocuous as it sounded. Austin had stressed that the homework—despite the fact that it was submitted online and it was open book—was meant to be an *individual* assignment. Doing it with someone else seemed to go directly against that order.

But all of that was too much to process or bring up at the moment. "Sure," he replied. *No use making things more difficult for now.*

Later that afternoon, Antonio had more time to think about it. The problem seemed mild enough, but the school had talked a lot about its Honor Code—and its one-strike-and-you're-out policy for any type of cheating. The code even claimed to create an obligation to report immediately to the professor any known instances of cheating or suffer similar consequences.

Antonio was lost, really. The way he saw things, the only way he could technically avoid breaking the code at this point was to report Ryan to the professor for proposing that they jointly work on homework. And that was out of the question—it would be the end of his brotherhood in the fraternity, and it didn't even feel like the right thing to do for such a minor issue.

Addressing The Cheating Culture

David Callahan, author of *The Cheating Culture*, suggests student cheating is related to the widespread cheating culture that has spread through all aspects of American life, including business, sports, and academe.[4] First, Callahan points to a "winner take all society," where the rewards for being the best can be so great that students will do whatever it takes to win. The payoffs of cheating are too great to ignore. Second, he links cheating to notions of fear and insecurity, pointing to the intense competition for scarce jobs or a place in an elite college or graduate school. Under these high-pressure conditions, many students feel as if one test could make the difference between a successful life and an ordinary one. In these circumstances, cheating is seen as a necessary evil. Third, Callahan notes that cheaters get away with their actions because no one is policing this behavior. This leads students to believe that they must cheat to keep up with their fellow students.

Others point to student over commitment as a reason for cheating. When sports, jobs, and other social commitments consume the student's time, the workload can become unmanageable. Cheating is seen as an escape. Research shows that panic cheating or cheating under duress increases when a student has a low grade point average or is under pressure to maintain a scholarship.[5]

Clearly over commitment was an issue for Antonio. His social life had created major sleep deficits, and he needed to keep his grades up to maintain his scholarship and eligibility status for athletics and stay off the fraternity's dog list. He had procrastinated on completing projects for other courses, and it appeared that cheating was the norm, even for the honors students. When he was confronted with the opportunity to access the treasure box of old exams, the lines between academic honesty and cheating became blurred for him.

Although Antonio had reservations about utilizing the old exams and working with Ryan on an *individual* homework assignment, he did what many students do when confronted with cheating—he rationalized the behavior. Is collaborating with another student on an individual assignment a minor issue? Is reviewing old tests really cheating? After all, no one would be harmed by his actions.

Peer influence to cheat may be the most powerful contributing factor to a culture of academic dishonesty on many campuses. One study found that students whose peers regularly cheat or whose peers consider cheating to be an acceptable practice are also more likely to engage in academic misconduct.[6] Peer acceptance of cheating appears to perpetuate the practice by evoking the behavior in other students.[7] Students often approach cheating as an accepted norm rather than an academic violation.[8] The student perception that cheating is the norm is very similar to the student perception that underage drinking and alcohol abuse are the norms for college students.

Another key factor contributing to student cheating is the instructor. First, most faculty members are hesitant to report incidents of academic dishonesty, which means that even students who are caught cheating continue to go unpunished.[9] There are a variety of factors that contribute to this reluctance, the most substantial of which is the burden of carrying out cumbersome hearing procedures.[10] If students notice their colleagues getting away with cheating, the legitimacy of the system is compromised, and those students will be more likely to view cheating as justified.

Research also reveals that students interpret leniency in policing exams as an implicit statement by the university that academic integrity is not all that important. When institutions turn a blind eye to violations of academic integrity, or the importance of honesty in the examination process is not stressed, students may see this almost as an invitation to cheat. It is clear the institution's attitude toward academic integrity can set the tone for the student body and either foster or constrain the cheating culture.

When students perceive their instructors to be indifferent about them—whether or not they learn the course material—students are more likely to cheat.[11] When Ryan told Antonio about the treasure box, he noted that "Austin's too damn lazy to actually come up with new tests every year." Whether Professor Austin is lazy or not is unknown; however, the perception of his students that he did not take the course seriously was persuasive and supported Ryan's position.

In a comprehensive study conducted by Donald L. McCabe in 2003, more than eighteen thousand students at twenty-three college campuses were surveyed on their attitudes toward cheating and plagiarism. Some of the students' anonymous comments are telling. One student noted, "If teachers taught better we wouldn't have to cheat."[12] Another student commented, "One time I downloaded a program off the Internet for my class. I hated the class and it was mandatory so I didn't care about learning it, just passing it."[13] Another student's perception of cheating is that "you can't stop it. . . . Some people were just raised that way—'do whatever you have to do.'"[14]

The way cheating has been trivialized by students demonstrates a disregard for core academic values and also a lack of civility. Cheating circumvents the learning process, skews academic measurement, and results in a misleading representation of actual attainment. Engaging in cheating also demonstrates disrespect for other students who actually work hard to achieve, professors who attempt to impart knowledge, and the academic community as a whole.

UNDERSTANDING PLAGIARISM

Of the many forms of academic misconduct, plagiarism is probably the most common. The English word *plagiarism* is derived from the Latin *plagiarius* ("kidnapper"), and *Black's Law Dictionary* defines it as "the deliberate and knowing presentation of another person's original ideas or creative expressions as one's own."[15] In its most basic sense, plagiarism is the verbatim copying (or cutting and pasting) of someone else's words without acknowledging the original author through use of quotation marks and proper citation. However, it can also be defined more broadly to include paraphrasing another author's work or borrowing someone else's original ideas without proper attribution. Thus, work that was produced in collaboration with other students could also be termed plagiarism when the professor has explicitly prohibited such cooperation.

The Internet has made plagiarism easier and more pervasive. Students can effortlessly copy and paste information from a website such as Wikipedia and incorporate it into their assignments without appropriate citation. Moreover, a number of websites allow students to purchase term papers, essays, and dissertations. Most students recognize these examples as blatant forms of plagiarism and understand the increased risks of being caught due to technological resources, such as Turnitin.com and SafeAssignment, which are widely used by colleges and universities to scan papers for plagiarism. Plagiarism can take on more nuanced forms, as Jacob discovered.

Jacob

It was only the fourth month of his eighteenth year on earth, but Jacob Douglas was pretty sure his world was about to end. On a Tuesday afternoon, he had done his normal routine of going by his campus mailbox, where he found a decidedly abnormal letter. He looked hard at the stern typeface, thinking that it had to be some sort of solicitation.

But it wasn't. Instead, it was a letter, which read,

Dear Mr. Douglas,

We regret to inform you that we have decided to begin a formal Honor Council investigation into your conduct in one of your classes. Specifically, one of your professors—who will remain anonymous for the time being—has provided evidence that you intentionally and maliciously used stolen, uncredited materials in order to finish an assignment. This is an allegation of the most serious magnitude and will be treated accordingly.

If you wish to contest these allegations, you must return this letter with a mark in the box labeled "I request a hearing." If you select that option, we will follow up this communication with more information about the proper procedures. But note that you **will not** be allowed to bring in any other person to provide assistance or evidence. The Honor Council believes that the best way to resolve this is to allow you to present your own side of the story in person and then let the merits govern.

Jacob was speechless. He literally had no idea what he possibly could have done wrong to merit such a terrible situation. He had been read the riot act on plagiarism frequently enough to be well acquainted with its evils and dangers, and he certainly hadn't meant to steal anyone else's ideas.

A few minutes of reflection started to clarify matters a little. As it turned out, the anonymous protections for the reporting professor were rather meaningless. His only substantive assignment so far was a small research paper he had done for his world history class on the Ming dynasty. Like most of his classmates, Jacob hadn't taken the assignment too seriously. Professor Thomson didn't seem likely to be all that harsh in grading all 120 ten-page papers for a class he obviously didn't enjoy teaching, so Jacob responded accordingly. He went to the library the night before the paper was due, pulled a few books off the shelf, hopped on Wikipedia for a while, and wrote a shallow paper on economic development in China in the seventeenth century.

But he did *write* it. While he had heard for years about the numbers of students who saw copying and pasting as the same as *writing* an assignment, he knew better than that. He had put together an original take on the subject with support from well-cited sources that he had reviewed. *Nothing wrong with that, right?*

By now he was starting to get a little angry. This was absolutely ridiculous—a charge he couldn't know anything more about, investigated in a process he had no part in by the same party that would decide his fate forever!

None of his options were especially appealing at that point. If Jacob abided by the terms of the letter, he would be stuck scrambling to defend himself against whatever evidence could be dug up against him, with no chance to prepare. The truth alone might not be enough. Of course, the other option would be to try to get some information in advance, but doing that would risk drawing the council's ire for possibly interfering with its investigation.

I'm screwed either way, he thought. *Might as well go down with a fight.*

After a restless night, he got ready in time the next morning to make it to Professor Thomson's office hours at 8:00. He was reasonably confident that no one else would be there—a combination of the facts that college students rarely get up at 8:00 in the morning and even more rarely attend professors' office hours before grades reach crisis level.

He was right. Glancing into the half-open door, he saw the lights down and no one but the professor sitting at his desk. He drew a breath and knocked softly.

"Come in," came the distracted reply.

Jacob took up the invitation and sat down. He waited a second for Professor Thomson to look up from the textbook he was reading.

"Mr. Douglas." It wasn't much of a greeting or a question.

"Dr. Thomson, I need to talk to you about my paper."

"Yes, I imagine you do."

"There seems to be some sort of confusion about it. I'm not at all sure what the deal is, but I wrote that paper myself. I made sure to cite my stuff, but the main ideas were mine."

"Really? It's certainly not the way it looked."

Jacob could detect the sarcasm in the professor's voice. "What do you mean?"

"All I know is that when I receive a paper that has facts taken straight from Wikipedia, it's one handed in by a cheater. Sorry to be blunt, but the circumstances speak for themselves."

Jacob was stunned. *Facts taken straight out of Wikipedia? Sure, I looked at it... and about a dozen other materials. And I cited most of them. But for facts?*

"But... but... what do you mean?"

"Oh, I suppose you magically knew the dates and names for everything you put in that script? I certainly don't believe *that*. You went somewhere for all the facts you included in the piece and didn't give credit even once."

Jacob was starting to feel his nervousness turn to anger. *Wait a second... this is crazy! If he's talking about dates and names, I saw those listed in at least half a dozen sources, none of which saw fit to cite an authority for them.*

Realizing that letting his first reply come out probably wouldn't help the situation, Jacob managed to keep an even tone. "I simply thought that the generally recognized historical facts were assumed to be widely known and didn't need a long citation for each and every one of them. Is that really a problem?"

"Look, Mr. Douglas, this is an issue for the Honor Council. I think any more questions you have need to go to them. Now, I need you to give me enough time to get ready for class."

Student Plagiarism—No Harm, No Foul

A growing body of research demonstrates that plagiarism is on the rise in American colleges and universities.[16] Colleges and universities across America and even around the world are seeing similar increases in academic dishonesty. Many attribute the rise in plagiarism to the pervasive use of electronic research, where with a click of a mouse, content can be easily cut and pasted into assignments and papers without proper citation.[17]

CAI research showed that 77 percent of students did not believe that cut-and-paste plagiarism was a serious issue.[18] Many students regard plagiarism as a matter of academic etiquette that should be avoided simply to escape punishment.[19] The perceived victimless nature of plagiarism may be one reason that students do not see it as a serious issue. If plagiarism is nothing more than impolite academic behavior, there is no real reason to avoid it other than to minimize the risk of punishment.

Another contributor to the surge in plagiarism is a lack of education—students do not understand what plagiarism encompasses. Complicating matters is that proper citation may vary based on certain disciplines and even among different professors. Jacob's alleged plagiarism would probably fall into this category. While Jacob did cite his sources, he may have unintentionally plagiarized by failing to cite sources for facts that he believed were common knowledge. Jacob's lack of clarity on what constitutes plagiarism, and perhaps his professor's failure to provide adequate instruction on what he considered plagiarism, resulted in a diversionary and perhaps avoidable hearing before the school's' Honor Council.

Communication can be one of the most effective methods of preventing plagiarism, particularly plagiarism resulting from improper citation. To reduce the confusion that can exist about proper citations, institutions may encourage faculty to adopt recognized writing styles, such as the Modern

Language Association (MLA) style, *Chicago Manual of Style*, or American Psychological Association (APA) style. Furthermore, when professors take the time to adequately educate and inform students about plagiarism within the context of an assignment, they may be able to prevent situations such as Jacob's from occurring. Just putting the university's plagiarism policy in the course syllabus is not enough to effectively prevent plagiarism, nor can it account for the range of nuanced requirements that differ among writing styles, instructors, and disciplines.

While Jacob's scenario involved an instance of unintentional plagiarism, many students plagiarize deliberately. They intentionally turn in someone else's work, cut and paste large sections of information from the Internet without using quotations or citing a source, and provide inadequate or incorrect citations. The root cause of this type of intentional plagiarism is laziness.

Despite honor codes and the threat of tough sanctions, many students choose to roll the dice and deliberately plagiarize in order to save time because they do not believe they will get caught. Detecting plagiarism can be a daunting task for a professor such as Jacob's, who had to read ten-page reports from 120 students. In this situation it is easy to see how student plagiarism could go undetected. New tools are available to help instructors detect plagiarism. For example, Turnitin.com is a Web-based system that scans student papers against 4.5 billion pages of books and journals in the ProQuest database and millions of documents already submitted through the system.[20] The system produces an originality report within minutes of submission that instructors can use to better identify instances of deliberate plagiarism.

In addition, some professors are taking low-tech measures to combat plagiarism, such as requiring some sources to have been published within the past year or to be from a prepared list. Instructors may set several intermediate deadlines along the way. If the student has to submit a topic proposal, preliminary research report, and rough draft before the final paper is due, it is less likely that the student will be able to procrastinate and pull something off the Internet at the last minute. Additionally, requiring an annotated bibliography—where the student must identify the source and where it was obtained and must reflect briefly on its applicability and reliability—ensures that the student will do independent research.

UNCIVIL PROFESSORS

The relationship between a student and a professor is a critical component of student learning. A professor's ability to transmit knowledge and promote inquiry based on research, study, and practical experience is one of the fundamental purposes of education. While most instructors are committed to free discussion and open inquiry, there have been growing concerns by students and commentators that some college classrooms are becoming platforms for political indoctrination where students are essentially attacked for reasoned views that are contrary to those of the instructor. This type of hostile behavior by professors is another example of incivility in the classroom.

Lindsey

As Lindsey strode into her 9:00 American government class, she gave a sigh. Professor Simpson had managed to recover from his threatening bout of bronchitis over the weekend, and there he was, sitting on top of the desk at the front of the classroom. To Lindsey, nothing could make her week worse. Eight weeks into her first semester of college, Simpson already represented all that was wrong in the world. His lunatic views on race relations inevitably took over every class, and he had lately identified Lindsey as his favorite sounding board for various ideas he knew would get a reaction.

She hadn't meant for any of this to happen. After a twenty-minute introduction the first day of class, she had simply become convinced that Professor Simpson was a genuine academician, opinionated, but open to opinions from others. With appropriate enthusiasm, she thought a lull in the first day's class—a discussion on presidential powers—was a good time to go back to something Simpson had said a minute ago. She quietly raised her hand.

Simpson looked up, a little surprised. "Yes, er, Ms. Singler. You have a question?"

"Just wanted clarification—what exactly did you mean when you said that the president's powers were premised on a racial hierarchy system of white supremacy? You just meant that the framers figured slavery to be part of the system when they designed it, right?"

Lindsey was patting herself on the back as she posed the question. It wasn't by any means her view of history or the structure of government, but she thought it gave a fair characterization of what Simpson was saying.

"Absolutely not. No! I meant *today's* system! The same system that you, Ms. Singler, probably voted to keep in the last election. The same system that you, your family, and the same country club, white Republicans have fought for years on end. Is that clear?"

Lindsey was too shocked to reply right away. The criticism was too sudden, too personal, for her to know what to say.

Apparently taking her silence as enough, Professor Simpson glanced over the large classroom of nervously shifting students and announced he was moving on.

But he didn't forget. Lindsey quickly became Simpson's favorite target whenever he was seeking a convenient foil for some of his topics. She first tried to be polite and demur, but eventually, she tired of rolling over and playing dead. She decided to fight back a little—always respectfully.

It all came to a head with the first assignment of the semester—a paper discussing the effect of slavery on the debates over the drafting of the Constitution. Lindsey thought about it quite a while and finally decided she'd go for broke; she'd argue—credibly, she thought, based on some of the books she checked out in the library—that the compromise accommodating slavery in the United States ultimately was a step in the right direction that could lead to a constitutional amendment to end the practice once and for all. She had no illusions about Simpson's likely reaction. To him, anything less than total damnation of the practice would reek of racism.

What she didn't expect was just how that reaction would show up in her grade. Despite being a paper that was coherent, well supported, and polished, it came back to her dripping red ink with a bold 56 printed on top. Lindsey was stunned; she had been an honors student all through high school, and the rest of her college grades so far pointed to academic success at the next level. While she recognized that she was far from Professor Simpson's favorite student, she still thought that she would have at least gotten a grade on the paper that reflected the work she put into it. Instead, hers was near the bottom of the class—lower than dozens that were obviously copied and pasted together the evening before.

What made it even worse was that she had no reason to expect a reprieve in the near future. The next grade in the class came on an assigned group project due in two weeks. Lindsey's group was given the task of preparing a brief presentation on the evolution of the American judiciary after the Civil War—not a challenging assignment, but one that would require some work.

She had enough sense to be cautious. The last thing she wanted to do was to have Professor Simpson's ire directed to her innocent group members and be reflected in their grade. Lindsey decided that the safest course of action would be to take the most nonobvious role in the group and do the final editing of the presentation and accompanying handout and only introduce the group when it was time for the presentation.

Things settled into a generally stable situation—although Lindsey was still very concerned about her grade—for a week. The following Monday, however, Jennifer pulled Lindsey aside after class.

"Look, Linz, you got to know this looks bad."

Lindsey looked at her in confusion. "What?"

"Your group participation. The others are getting kind of pissed that you're not doing your fair share. I've tried to make them happy, but it's not working."

She hadn't seen this one coming. Lindsey never planned to be skipping out of work—in fact, it was nothing like her to even be accused of it. *But if grades are on the line*, she thought, *everyone gets edgy. Wish they had talked to me first, but I need to see how to fix it.*

Student Academic Freedom in the Classroom

Professors often rely on their right to academic freedom to justify particular actions taken in the classroom, including how they evaluate students. Faculty academic freedom typically includes the right to study, discuss, investigate, teach, and publish. At public colleges and universities, academic freedom is a constitutional right, closely associated as a by-product of the First Amendment. At private institutions, academic freedom is generally a contractual right. However, what are the rights of a student such as Lindsey, when a professor's academic freedom creates a hostile learning environment or results in an unfair assessment? Some commentators have referred to this issue as a form of "freedom of expression" or "intellectual diversity," and the media have given it attention in recent years.

Clearly, students do have rights. Professor Simpson's brash, unfair, and personally demeaning conduct would most likely not be covered under any academic freedom protections. Courts have consistently found that academic freedom does not give faculty members the right to say or do whatever they want in the classroom. Specifically, academic freedom does not protect a faculty member who compromises a student's right to learn in an environment free of hostility or engages in controversial speech unrelated to the course.[21] As a result, courts have held that professors have no right to use profanity in class unless it is germane to the subject matter and that they have no First Amendment right to determine what they will teach in the classroom if it is counter to university policy.

Furthermore, one of the professional guidelines established by the American Association of University Professors (AAUP) recommends that professors should "encourage free discussion, inquiry, and expression" and that "students should be free to take reasoned exception to the data or views offered in any course of study."[22] The recommendation further suggests that "students should have protection through orderly procedures against prejudiced or capricious academic evaluation."[23] Unfortunately, Lindsey was not afforded these protections.

While there are few comprehensive studies that assess the scope of the issues that Lindsey encountered, there are reports of similar inappropriate and uncivil conduct by professors across the United States. For example, a report released in 2009 by the American Council of Trustees and Alumni (ACTA) cites a case in which a social work student was required to sign a letter supporting gay adoption as part of a class project, which was against the student's religious beliefs.[24] The student's failure to sign the letter drastically affected the student's grade. According to David Horowitz, founder of Students for Academic Freedom, a history professor at a prestigious Ivy League school welcomed his class with the warning that he had strong liberal opinions and that Republican students should drop his course.[25] According to the Students for Academic Freedom, it has collected hundreds of similar student stories of alleged ideological discrimination that has occurred in college classrooms.[26]

The second problem that Lindsey encountered is a familiar one for college students: group assignments. Group assignments appear in an increasingly large portion of college syllabi, reflecting the growing need for collaboration in the workplace or the crushing workload faced by professors grading individual assignments—or some combination of the two. These sorts of group projects almost inevitably invite fears of uncivil conduct, if not the behavior itself. No matter how "individualized" grading is in theory, in practice the final group project has the strongest bearing on the group grade, notwithstanding the risk of shirking.

Here, Lindsey is facing the displeasure of her fellow group members for the perception that she is not pulling her fair share of the weight. In her case, this appears to be the result of poor communication from the outset. Failure to strictly assign roles in a group setting at the very beginning of the project sets the groundwork for miscommunication and potential problems of perception down the road. Considerate conduct would be addressing these concerns before they develop into outright hostility.

Often, complaints about uncivil conduct in the group setting have an even stronger basis in fact. College students who shirk on their work may take advantage of the opportunity because of competing obligations, ranging from part-time jobs to service projects to social organizations or downright laziness and inconsiderate conduct. Deliberately shirking on work is not civil conduct because it shows a disregard for others. Professors would be well advised to fight this particular type of incivility by focusing on developing more sophisticated individualized grading mechanisms, such as having group members grade each other's contributions. Students can benefit from clearly defined expectations and roles at the outset and clarifications that excessive shirking is not just detrimental, but might give rise to communications with professors and impact grades.

UNCIVIL STUDENTS

Student incivility toward professors is increasing. Professors complain that students disrupt class by carrying on running conversations, texting, reading the newspaper, eating, watching television, and not turning off their cell phones. Furthermore, it is not uncommon for students to aggressively challenge a professor's authority, ability to teach, and the way a teacher grades assignments. This conduct is disruptive and diversionary, and it creates a negative work environment for the professor and the other students.

Sonam

Sonam's first few weeks of college had gone pretty smoothly. Other than the normal transitions—for which she was mostly prepared—nothing of note seemed to come up. Her classes, which were all part of the university's core curriculum and spoon-fed in large classes, some taught by graduate students, were easy enough and not interfering too much with life in general.

Spanish was a bit of a problem, though. Although Sonam certainly had no trouble keeping up with the study—three years of Spanish class in high school definitely helped—she never could feel too comfortable in the classroom. And that was all because of Ms. (or Senorita, as she preferred) Williams.

Ms. Williams was a youngish graduate student who had decided—either by default or by naïve enthusiasm—to take on teaching responsibilities for a small section of Spanish 1000. She probably went into it believing that it would be a good opportunity to add some shine to her resume while also earning some meager additional income. She was quite shocked to discover the additional toll that teaching would take on her.

The class was comprised of various interconnected cliques—fraternity brothers, sorority sisters, and other friends—and Ms. Williams was quite at a loss to know how to engage them. As a result, from day one, the students in Spanish 1000, section 011, had decided that they—and not the demur Ms. Williams—were going to control the class

It started innocuously enough, Sonam recalled. The first day of class, the students decided it would be fun to mess with the seating chart. Along with the surprise attendance of Yosemite Sam and Speedy Gonzales in the class, Ms. Williams realized at the end of the day that the last names of all of her students were mixed up on her roll—or so she thought at first.

At the time, Sonam had gone along with the joke. It just seemed like innocent fun, and she didn't want to be the obviously prudish freshman. But the more subtle forms of disrespect didn't end on the first day. Some of the guys in the class took only a week to develop the habit of referring to Ms. Katherine Williams as "Kat"; first to everyone else, then gradually to her face. At first, she smiled, taking the familiarity as a compliment, and she mildly corrected them from using it. But as time wore on, Sonam saw that it was used more tactically by almost all of the students of the class. It was a term that removed one of the formal separations of student and teacher. Ms. Williams had noticed this as well.

At first, it looked like she made a bold effort to avoid letting it get to her. Instead of smiling at her name, she quickly corrected the offending student—always to a surprised, if disingenuous, apology. But the student's' behavior didn't stop there. By the midterm, the class had managed to guilt-trip Ms. Williams into waiving their three lowest homework grades (out of eight) and giving them a study guide that essentially included all the answers to the midterm. The students (maybe accurately) pointed out that these were standard practices in other classes and (not accurately) that Williams was not being fair or teaching the material effectively enough to hold them up to the standards set out in the class syllabus.

By October, Sonam was miserable with this arrangement. *Really? This is what they want out of a college class?* she wondered. She certainly didn't have any delusions of grandeur about the university or the motives of its students. *But still—we're paying good money each semester to sit in a classroom, wasting time and harassing a poor teacher who would rather just get her degree and get out of here.*

Despite her frustrations with Spanish class, Sonam had more pressing issues to deal with that week. Three weeks before, she had taken part in Take Back the Night, a protest sponsored by one of the women's groups on campus that was designed to raise awareness of sexual violence and the measures needed to be taken to combat it. Sonam was an enthusiastic supporter of the idea, and she volunteered to work a table on the concourse for a two-hour block that afternoon.

For the most part, it was a dull assignment. She had been warned that it might be slow on a Tuesday during classes, but Sonam didn't realize how slow. That's why she was shocked to see a group of guys suddenly approach her from one of the classroom buildings.

"What's this all about?" one asked.

Sonam hesitated a second. The tone wasn't exactly friendly, but she didn't want to sound defensive, either. "It's a women's violence thing," she started. "We just think…"

"Yeah, figured it was something like that," the second interrupted. "Look—we've been watching you from class for the last forty minutes, and we just had to get over here."

"This bullshit has to stop," the first demanded. "I know what this is all about—propaganda about how it's always the guy's fault, how 99 percent of all college girls claim to have been raped. All I see is more women out there spreading this Ya-Ya message about how guys are pigs and rapists. And it's just not right!"

Sonam had managed to keep from looking too shocked at the moment, but she was absolutely stunned. She didn't have any idea who these guys were, but the situation was incredibly uncomfortable. And unfair! *I haven't done a thing to one of them… and they think they can just come over here and treat me like this.* She felt her face turning red.

Apparently, the third guy started to detect it. Some of the initial fury had subsided, and he managed to start in a calmer voice than his buddies: "All we're saying is that we think you're working for a group that's unfair and that's essentially lying about guys everywhere. We can't do anything on campus without catching the guilt-trip routine, and our parties get constant harassment when some girl gets drunk and gets left by her friends. We just want you all to quit spreading the propaganda and making it worse."

"Is there a problem here?"

Sonam almost died with relief to see Dr. Randolph walk up to the table. Dr. Randolph served as adviser to the group sponsoring the event and apparently knew enough to keep a close eye on things.

"Uh, no. Nothing," guy two managed to say. They were still mad but seemed to recognize that the situation had changed enough to make a quick getaway the best option. The three turned and started to walk off quietly, throwing a couple of angry glances back over their shoulders.

"Are you alright Ms. Kumar?" Dr. Randolph asked Sonam. "I'm okay," said Sonam as she tried to regain her composure.

"What was that all about?" Dr. Randolph asked.

"I don't even know," Sonam replied. "They seemed to take issue with… something, not even sure what, and decided to come take it out on me. Thanks for scaring them off." At that point, Sonam was still a bit mad, but beginning to cool down. It wasn't something worth getting upset over.

"Did they threaten you? Make you feel uncomfortable?"

"Uh… well, yeah. I mean, they definitely made me feel uncomfortable. I don't know if they threatened me…"

But Dr. Randolph had heard enough and missed the last sentence. "This is ridiculous! They can't get away with stuff like this! And I recognized the short blond one—he was in my psychology class a few semesters ago. I'm going right now to look up his name."

Sonam was a little confused. *It's over, right?* she thought. *Wasting time on these guys is giving them too much credit.*

Dr. Randolph must have noticed Sonam's expression. "Sonam, you have a right not to be accosted. No one can just come up to you and say things like that! I'm going to turn those idiots over to the administration for violating the Anti-Harassment Pledge."

Sure, the guys were being obnoxious, but they seemed worked up over something due to ignorance of the situation, not actual malice. And they hadn't actually threatened to do anything to *her*—or even said much about her. They had chosen to express their opinion—loudly and not nicely—but just an opinion.

Even an accusation of violating the Anti-Harassment Pledge had pretty dire consequences. Sonam had been in a smallish English class with one guy who was rumored to have transferred after hearing that the school was looking into some misogynistic posters he had put up inside his dorm room. She couldn't swear that was the truth, but she did know that his seat had sat empty every day for the last two weeks.

Later that evening, as she tried to focus on doing a little homework, Sonam couldn't help but wonder what had happened earlier. She didn't know exactly *what* she felt. Sure, it was awful to have been the target of such obnoxious behavior. But she was a big girl, and she thought she had made it to the real world now that she was off on her own at school. She wasn't much of a fan of imagining the "politeness police" sticking up for her rights.

Speech And Civility Codes

Colleges and universities have responded to the rise in incivility among students, students and professors, and students and the outside community by developing speech codes meant to encourage students to treat others with respect and anti-harassment codes ostensibly meant to protect students from harassment. These codes broadly prohibit conduct, including speech that would intimidate or harass people with certain characteristics. These codes often explicitly provide that violators will be subject to the school's disciplinary process.

Speech codes often include language indicating that students are subject to sanction if they disrupt class. Some institutions have developed guidelines for faculty to follow to address disruptive students who persistently arrive late or leave early, talk incessantly while a professor is delivering a lecture, or become disrespectful or belligerent when confronted about their behavior, as Sonam observed in her Spanish class.

These types of guidelines allow professors to take disciplinary action when such behavior "interferes with the learning process for other students, inhibits the ability of instructors to teach most effectively, diverts energy . . . away from the education mission, and indicates a significant level of personal problems . . . on the part of the disrupter."[27]

General civility codes are a more modern creation and have sprung up in great numbers over the last few years.[28] The language of these codes speaks to a respect for diversity of opinions and a respect for the rights of others in general. These codes do not explicitly prohibit any behavior, but are often aspirational in nature. Civility codes may include behavioral expectations for students by encouraging courteous and dignified interactions that are marked by consideration and tolerance of others' ideas. Some schools have civility projects with courses on civility and regular presentations to students that focus on civility.

Many institutions have both civility codes and harassment policies. For instance, the civility code at the University of California, Berkeley states that it expects students to consult the student code for specific regulations regarding respect and civility. The Berkeley student code includes sections on "Protected Group Harassment Policies" and regulations setting up designated areas for free expression. The harassment policy allows the school to impose discipline for, among other acts, harassing activities such as "the use, display, or other demonstration of words, gestures, imagery, or physical materials . . . that has the effect of creating a hostile and intimidating environment sufficiently severe or pervasive to substantially impair" a minority's participation in the university.[29]

While a college civility code is unlikely to change dramatically the way that students interact on campus, it does establish a baseline behavioral expectation in the community.

4

A school without football is in danger of deteriorating into a medieval study hall.

—Frank Leahy

COLLEGE ATHLETICS

Every Saturday in the fall, the state of Alabama experiences a huge demographic shift. Tens of thousands of people make a weekly commute to two small cities on the opposite sides of the state, temporarily transforming them into some of the largest metropolises in the region. Fans—including over half the undergraduate student population of the universities—pile into the massive stadiums for a nearly religious experience of watching, feeling, and drinking in a football game.

While football might be the behemoth in Alabama, basketball reigns supreme just a few hours to the east. Students at the University of North Carolina and Duke University put their time, enthusiasm, and talent into showing the most passionate support for their teams—and in making the most hostile environment possible for the other team. Students at Duke live in tents in "Krzyzewskiville"—named for their beloved coach Mike Krzyzewski—for months before major home basketball games in order to ensure they get seats.

In any way you picture it, college athletics is a big business. Pulling in more than $60 billion a year in revenues, sports at the university level touch on every part of the college universe, from student life to academics to administrative priorities.[1] Whether a student has any interest at all in a certain sport has little relevance to whether the university's decisions about the sports have an impact on the student.

In dealing with college athletics, university administrators face tough challenges. After all, the revenue-producing sports—primarily football and basketball—are a profitable business at many universities and thus aid the institution in its education mission. In this sense, universities feel pressures to maximize profits in selected sports and thus compensate for funding shortfalls in other sports.

But the question now facing administrators is whether the big sports, big money culture that has evolved at many universities makes the money worth it. Students have shown a marked tendency toward uncivil behavior, ranging from skipping classes on Fridays because they interfere with tailgating plans to rioting after close losses and sometimes victories as well. Universities have also shown questionable judgment in placing athletics as a priority in admissions and budgeting, treating students unfairly and uncivilly. All of this can be tied in part to the modern big money athletics culture on college campuses.

A BRIEF HISTORY

Organized college athletics did not exist before the Civil War.[2] Colleges had slowly branched away from their original narrow focus on instructing their students in strictly intellectual and spiritual fields, but had not yet conceived of the idea of organized physical contests as contributing to college life.

By the 1830s, promoting student health had become one goal of American colleges, which began to add gymnasiums in an effort to further that goal—and to divert energies that had been used in pranks and misbehavior directed at professors and administrators.[3] But perhaps for the same reasons that students resented many of the formal parts of education, they resented paternalistic tendencies in promoting health, and the gym-building movement ended within a decade.

By the 1840s, students had begun to play several popular ball games on campus in unofficial, pickup game fashion. Boat clubs, organized for competitive rowing, offered some intercollegiate competition, but students appeared to lack the sense of urgency and competitiveness that animates modern athletic competition.

All of this changed over the next several decades. A movement promoting sports and athleticism took off at American universities, leading to the incorporation of organized leagues for crew, baseball, track and field, and football by the 1870s.

Early sports were rowdy and dangerous affairs, suffering from a lack of standardized rules and protective equipment. In 1905 alone, eighteen men died from playing organized football on college campuses.[4] Sensing the need for reform, President Theodore Roosevelt called on college coaches and administrators to initiate reforms in the game of football, the most visible and dangerous collegiate sport.

College administrators responded to calls for reform of all college athletics by meeting in December 1905 and forming the Intercollegiate Athletic Association of the United States, the forerunner of today's National Collegiate Athletic Association, more commonly known as the NCAA. Although only thirty-nine institutions—and few of the contemporary powerhouses in the game of football—initially signed on with the organization, it quickly gained momentum and achieved the dominant position as the administrator of college athletics that it still holds today.

While the administrative body at the top of college sports has been constant over the past century, the sports themselves have been anything but. More than anything else, improved technology—both in the forms of the media, from radio to modern satellite television, and in improved means of transportation—has revolutionized college athletics. In 2009, NCAA college football teams sold more than forty-three million tickets.[5] One hundred and thirty million viewers tuned in to watch the NCAA Division I College Basketball Championship in 2008.[6]

Collegiate athletics is a big and complicated business. No one disputes that. The tough questions arise in the more subtle issues that come with college sports.

STUDENT ATHLETES

College sports are a major contributor to campus culture, identity, and pride. Students, alumni, and the entire campus community passionately rally around their school's athletic teams in hopes of winning the big game or, more important, a conference title or national championship.

The success of an institution's athletic teams, especially the highly popular NCAA Division I men's football and basketball teams, may produce millions in television revenue and spotlight national attention.

Data suggest that the success of an institution's athletic teams may bolster undergraduate admissions as well as giving.[7]

Even institutions with less prestigious Division III athletic programs are able to benefit from offering students opportunities to participate in collegiate sports. While these institutions may not get the big money and notoriety associated with Division I athletic programs, they are able to use their teams as a recruitment tool for athletes who want to continue to play at the collegiate level.[8]

With so much riding on the success of an institution's athletic programs, colleges and universities aggressively recruit elite high school athletes from around the country and take steps to make sure star players remain eligible to play. The preferential treatment given to student athletes has created issues of civility, especially when schools turn a blind eye to academic and behavioral misconduct by student athletes.

Antonio

"Johnson? Johnson? Is Marcus here?"

Nope, Antonio thought. *Just like Chad and DeMario. Just like last week.*

Friday, 9:00 a.m. sociology class had proved to be the bane of the baseball team. Most of the players took the "only losers party on the weekend" mantra to heart—Thursdays were notorious nights for bangers. Antonio had gone to one last night, but feeling a little sick, he made sure he made it back to his room by 1:00 a.m.

The problem was that everyone else on the team knew two things. First, they knew that Antonio *would* be in class on Friday mornings. While certainly not the most dedicated student, he had decided a while ago that simply showing up went a long way. But with that came a price—notes and heads-ups to team members. After all, he didn't want to be the "little bitch that ruined it for everyone," as Chad had so eloquently put it the other night. Antonio wasn't thrilled with the arrangement, but he figured he could deal with it. If that's what it took to keep the older players happy and off his back, he could handle it.

The second fact bothered him a bit more. The players on the team knew that Coach Miller wouldn't let any of his players fail a class. How exactly he handled that was still somewhat of a mystery. Sure, he had read some guys the riot act once or twice, trying to instill the fear of God in them about the danger of failing. But that didn't solve every problem.

Everyone on the team knew that Coach Miller had no qualms about wandering into the Central Building West corridor and hunting down individual professors to ask them about his players' grades. He never threatened, never yelled, never made serious suggestions. But he sure could talk. A big, powerful man with an iron handshake and a big smile, he would sit down with even the most stoic literature professor and talk him into terms. Terms could be something as simple as better guidelines for an upcoming project (to be passed right on to the designated athletic tutors, of course) or something as extreme as additional credits through independent study for team members falling behind on hours. Antonio didn't know what all was involved with it, but he *did* know that it sure seemed to be an attractive option for the seniors on the team: over half of them had earned hours through the Psychology Department through supervised research in the past year.

Antonio managed to pry his eyelids open for the remaining fifty minutes of class. Thoughts of his plans for the weekend filled his mind. There was a big football game tomorrow, and he had been drafted as part of the group for hosting high school football and baseball recruits who were planning to attend. After touring the campus during the day, several of them had made arrangements to spend a night in the dorms with some current athletes and experience the school from the inside.

He really was stoked about it. His visit last year had really sealed the deal on his selection, even if he didn't have a ton of options, he admitted to himself. Just hanging out with the people on the team and finding out that they were normal, chill people who shared a lot in common with him went a long way to selling him on the school.

Antonio went back to his room, took a nap, and took care of some homework for the rest of the day. At 4:30 he showed up as scheduled and met Taylor, a football recruit, who would be his guest for the night. Also there for the visit were Taylor's mom and younger sister; Antonio greeted them all with a friendly smile and enough assurances that he'd "keep her son out of trouble" to put the mom's heart at some state of ease.

No sooner had Antonio and Taylor turned to head back to the dorms than the tone of the conversation changed quite a bit. "So, what kind of action you got on tap for us tonight?" asked Taylor with a big smile on his face.

Antonio had to hold back a laugh. He remembered what it was like to be the star of the evening and to be exposed to the wide world of college for the first time. *He's just a kid. I'll try to make sure he has a good time.*

"Hell, man, not that much. We'll just hang out for a while—got a Wii in the dorm. There's a couple of parties starting around nine that we can hit up."

Antonio's plan was simple. He and Taylor would experience a normal night together. They might go out, hang with some people, whatever. But it would be pretty low key.

He had given some thought to some of the concerns of getting into trouble. Parties would mean alcohol available to everyone, and he'd either have to let Taylor make the call whether he'd drink or play the very uncool role of parent and keep him from drinking at all. The university had told them quite clearly that alcohol was off limits, but the coaches had added their own message that recruiting was a huge deal and that they were to do whatever it took—which Antonio took as a wink at some of the tighter restrictions. He figured he'd play it as it went.

Taylor had different plans. "A party? Like just a frat party or something? Better be some hot bitches there. There sure were at the one I went to last week."

"Ha, yeah, I'm sure there will be," Antonio replied. "Plenty here on campus."

Taylor looked at him with a small grin on his face. "No, man, I don't think you know what I'm saying. *Last* week we partied with some hot girls—not the kind you usually find on campus. The kind you stick a dollar at."

Antonio laughed off this comment and changed the subject. But his mind stayed on it for a while. *Really? Strippers? Just so some damned cocky kid will come to your school?* Apparently, recruiting was an even crazier world than he realized.

Recruitment

From the onset, many student athletes are treated like rock stars. For example, before a student athlete selects a college or university, it is very likely that coaches or representatives from a number of institutions have made contacts with the student in an attempt to secure enrollment. The recruitment process for top athletes is highly competitive, and institutions have been known to take extraordinary measures to entice enrollment.[9]

While the NCAA has established rules that govern the recruitment process, over the years institutions have found creative ways to circumvent restrictions, and some have been caught. A common recruitment violation is for coaches and boosters to offer additional benefits, over and above scholarships, to student athletes and their families. The NCAA has sanctioned institutions for supplying student athletes with additional benefits such as large cash gifts under the table, special trips, and loaner vehicles.[10]

One recruitment mechanism commonly used by institutions is to invite recruits for an official campus visit. These visits, authorized by the NCAA during certain periods, give student athletes an opportunity to meet with players, coaches, and staff and experience a prospective school from the inside out. These visits can be very influential in a student's decision-making process. Antonio's visit as a recruit had helped sell him on enrollment.

As Antonio experienced, coaches may put pressure on student hosts to show recruits a good time, which may put players in an awkward position. Antonio quickly discovered that showing someone a good time meant more than just hanging out in a dorm playing video games. For many recruits a good time means access to wild parties, alcohol, and sex. Coaches and athletic departments cannot officially condone such behavior when recruits visit; however, evidence suggests that some recognize the expectations and indirectly encourage players to entertain recruits in ways that meet over-the-top expectations.[11]

For example, in a lawsuit involving the University of Colorado's football recruitment program, the court noted that the coach resisted reforms to questionable recruitment practices, which unofficially involved providing recruits with alcohol, drugs, and sexual encounters with drunken female students. The coach claimed that "at schools all over the country recruits were shown 'a good time,' met young women, and went to parties, and if such activities weren't allowed at CU, it would be a 'competitive disadvantage' for the football team."[12] In a competitive environment, the entertainment options provided to student athletes may be very influential and could tip the scales.

The recruitment process may actually perpetuate systemic incivility in student athletes. When university coaches indirectly encourage players to engage in conduct that violates university policy to induce enrollment, the message to athletes is that they are exempt from the law. Several studies have found that student athletes are more likely than other students to binge drink, use illicit drugs, and commit sexual assaults.[13] Even when athletes are reported for uncivil conduct such as sexual assault, punishments tend to be very light or nonexistent.[14] This further reinforces the untouchable status of student athletes and may encourage more misconduct and incivility.

Maintaining Eligibility

Student athletes are supposed to be students first and athletes second. To ensure that athletes focus on academics, the NCAA has set a number of academic requirements that student athletes must meet to be eligible to play. Student athletes must achieve a certain SAT score, pass specific core classes, and maintain a minimum grade point average. Furthermore, the NCAA requires that athletes demonstrate progress toward a degree to remain eligible to play; athletes must complete a percentage of their degree requirement every year with a minimum grade point average.[15]

Institutions have been known to engage in academic fraud to help athletes meet eligibility requirements to play—anything from tutors writing athletes' papers or taking tests for athletes to players' passing bogus courses.[16] In some cases the pervasiveness of the academic fraud has even implicated senior administrators.[17] The notion that a college or university would engage in academic fraud to ensure athlete eligibility demonstrates another systemic incivility.

Antonio wondered how his coach was able to negotiate terms with individual faculty members to help varsity players attain academic eligibility. The coach was able to facilitate special academic accommodations that ranged from giving athletic tutors insider information on exams to allowing student athletes to complete additional projects for extra credit.

THE FANS—LOVE THY ENEMY

A visiting team and its fans can expect a certain degree of incivility during a home game. The home team's fans will do their best to disrupt the concentration of the visiting team by taunting, jeering, and making noise. Depending on the importance of the game and the rivalry between the competing teams, the level and intensity of hostilities of the home team's fans will vary. Sometimes fan excitement can get out of control.

Lindsey

Lindsey was the first one up in her dorm on Saturday morning at the ungodly hour of 9:00. She took a look out the window and grinned. Eighty degrees and sunny. Perfect weather for her first college football game.

Everything had gone exactly as planned. The cute boy from Sigma had asked her to be his date to the game, and she now had social plans from sunup to sundown on Saturday. *So glad I'm not stuck going with Megan.* The roommates got along great, but each knew the horror of being stuck at a football game without the proper company of a fraternity brother.

Lindsey got up and got dressed, putting on the new sundress and espadrilles she had saved for the day. The dress was her uniform, so to speak. Only the Greek students thought that sweat, bourbon, and football went well with lawn party attire.

By 11:00, Lindsey had wandered over to the Sigma house where the brothers would be tailgating. At this point, it was still pretty quiet. A few of the alums had arrived and started setting up televisions and grills, but almost none of the brothers had managed to recover from a rough night yet. Lindsey found Lisa, a girl in her sorority, grabbed a bottle of water, and started to chat eagerly about the day.

Before too long, the Sigma brothers began drifting out of the recesses of the house and onto the lawn. They, too, wore the uniform of the day, khakis and logoed button-down shirts, and everyone wore sunglasses. Whether they were intended more to hide the sun or to hide the wearer wasn't clear.

Thomas, Lindsey's date for the game, came out. He was a nice guy, a few years older than Lindsey, but only a year ahead in school. They had met at a swap a few weeks ago, but this would be the first time they spent significant time together. Thomas noticed her and made his way over. The two quickly got caught up in conversation while the early conference game blared on the newly set-up television in the background. The tailgate had begun.

The afternoon melted away. As the hours went on, Lindsey noticed that the crowd grew louder, but not bigger. She had the sense to suspect that it was the coolers of light beer that kept popping up in an almost endless supply. Figuring she might as well join in, she grabbed a can and a cup.

"Hey, whoa, what are you doing?" Thomas's sudden question startled her, and Lindsey turned.

"Just thought I might as well…" Lindsey trailed off.

Thomas looked hesitant. *Cute,* thought Lindsey. *But I'm a big girl—he doesn't have to look out for me.*

"Look, I don't care if you get buzzed. But the deal is that you're getting to hang out with the fraternity because you'll take care of me when I'm drunk later on. If you can't handle that, you won't be back. Okay?"

Lindsey frowned. Sure, she had known that the usual practice was that the girls dragged their intoxicated dates around all day and made sure that nothing terrible—i.e., nothing involving the police or a fight—happened. But she didn't at all expect it to be so ugly and blunt.

"Sure. Just one. You might like me better this way, anyway." Lindsey managed a smile. No reason to let this ruin the perfect day.

The din continued uninterrupted other than the occasional shout of glee or despair in response to the events on the television. Although everyone was getting a little rowdy, it seemed to be the right time and place for it—at a frat house, outside on a game day. Plus, it might come in handy to have some buzzed fans in the stands come kickoff.

"Whatcha doing, you crazy blue bastard?" came the bellowing taunt from a few feet away. On the sidewalk heading toward campus, a couple of college students decked out in blue and obviously here for the visitors turned, grinned, and stuck a prominent middle finger at the brothers. Several of them laughed, but one—a young kid named Spencer—didn't take so kindly to it.

"I want to rip your heads off! You will be crying the whole way back home!"

The outburst startled those around him, but the crowd quickly laughed and went back to its business. Lindsey would have laughed, too, except she couldn't help seeing two families walking down the sidewalk at the moment, each hurrying their kids past the house. *Aw, no need for that*, she thought.

An hour before kickoff, the party was packing up. The fraternity brothers went back into the house and came out with armfuls of mini bourbons and vodkas and started passing them out to the crowd.

"Ha, how are you going to get that in? Stick it down your pants?" Lindsey teased Thomas.

Thomas grinned at her. "I'm not," he said. "You are. Part two of being a football date."

Lindsey looked around. The other girls were already starting to hike up their dresses and apply masking tape around their thighs. *Even more than I bargained for*, she thought.

The Fans

A discussion of civility in the context of an intercollegiate athletic competition may seem futile. A modest level of uncivil conduct is almost inherent to athletic competitions. Moreover, fan enthusiasm is one of the many factors that make sporting events so much fun. However, when the teams are collegiate and alcohol is involved, enthusiasm can easily cross the line into violence. This is why a 2005 *USA Today* survey found that 69 percent of all colleges and universities ban the sale of alcohol at sporting events.[18]

Even with alcohol restrictions, students find creative ways to get a buzz before and even during sporting events. The tailgate party is one of the most famous pre-game rituals observed by college football fans around the country. The beverage of choice for these events is beer, although any alcoholic beverage will do. Intoxication before the game is the goal. Students may also sneak alcoholic beverages into sporting events, as Lindsey quickly learned.

During Lindsey's first college football game as a student and sorority sister, she experienced firsthand questionable student norms before the game and ways that fan enthusiasm can quickly deteriorate. Alcohol consumption is a centerpiece for many student game day activities. According to the Harvard School of Public Health's College Alcohol Study, student sports fans binge drink more than students who are not fans.[19] This excessive drinking leads to secondhand effects, such as violence.

Alcohol clearly loosens fans up before the game; however, at the party Lindsey attended, one fan was a bit too loose. It is one thing to talk a little trash to an opposing team's fans, but comments such as "I want to rip your heads off" are very provocative. Such comments could have escalated into an all-out brawl had the visiting fans chosen to respond more aggressively. Such uncivil altercations ignore the sensibilities of others, such as families with small children, who attend sporting events.

ABUSIVE FANS

When thousands of fans come together to root for their team in a ballpark, stadium, or arena, the energy is palpable. College sports are no exception. Nineteen of the twenty largest stadiums located in the United States are devoted to college football.[20] Many of these stadiums can hold more than one hundred thousand screaming fans. In 2009, more than twenty-five million fans attended a NCAA Division I men's basketball game, and several teams drew more than twenty thousand fans per game.[21] Sometimes the excitement and energy of an athletic competition can cause fan enthusiasm to turn into uncivil fan abuse.

Sonam

By the time November rolled around, Sonam was totally pumped. She had managed to stay out of the hysteria of football season and focus on school for the first few months, but basketball was a different story entirely. Sonam had shown enough enthusiasm and creativity to win the audition for tickets in student block seating, guaranteeing her a spot in the wildest part of the arena for every home game.

The season was off to a good start. The Falcons had cruised through their nonconference schedule unscathed and now looked poised to make a run at the conference title. This Thursday night brought a key divisional matchup against their hated in-state rival.

The students were prepared. A week before the game, the opposing team's small starting forward's phone number had hit a Facebook fan site. Chaos ensued. Taunts came in every size and package—late night phone calls and text messages, all unwelcome, most profane, and some downright frightening. Sonam had seen the post and sent a quick text—one she actually regretted for its lack of creativity—but didn't think any more about it.

At tip-off, the arena was absolutely alive with energy. The cheers drowned out the stadium announcers as the players made their way onto the court. Everyone in the arena was ready for an intense game.

But the crowd wasn't ready for what happened next. As the opposing team's starting lineup was announced, the student section sat rather quietly—unusual for a group that had no qualms about being rowdy when necessary. But when the fourth player's name came over the speakers, the students roared on cue: "Raa-pist. Raa-pist. Raa-pist."

Coordination, communication, and creativity had struck again. Apparently, the player—a gangly kid who looked too young to be on the court—had a minor run-in with the police about a sexual assault claim in high school. Charges were never filed, and the situation seemed to be no big deal. But it was on Google, and that made all the difference. The student fans had found it in the dark reaches of the Internet and used the vast communication resources at their disposal—Twitter, Facebook, and texting—to efficiently coordinate an attack of the most devastating kind.

The jeer set the tone for the entire evening. The game was an ugly, physical match with plenty of personal and technical fouls called on each side. The fans reacted accordingly, growing more vindictive with every call until the whole place was shaking.

It all came to a head with 1:58 left in the second half. The Falcons' starting forward set his feet in the lane to block a drive to the basket and inexplicably got called for his fifth and final foul. The place exploded with pent-up frustration. Sonam furiously jumped into the crowd's cadence of "Bullshit! Bullshit!"

She didn't join the next part of the crowd's reaction, however. Out of the corner of her eye, Sonam watched a full water bottle launch out of the hand of a red-faced young man wearing a backwards hat and smack an opposing player in his back. A cup—half full of ice and who knows what— also flew onto the court, showering everyone in its trajectory.

At this point the crowd was just mad—at each other, at the referees, at its own team, everyone. One soaked guy near the front had climbed up a few rows while shouting for the punk who threw the cup to come down and face him. Others were shoving and pushing, gradually expanding down to the edges of the court. Recognizing the situation, the referees instantly blew the whistle and pushed the players down into the entrance tunnel—wisely doing it one team at a time.

What is going on? thought Sonam. The fracas around her had managed to steer her thoughts away from the game for a while. *It is a game, after all. And we are supposedly adults. But this looks more like a kindergarten display.*

After twenty minutes of sorting things out, play resumed, and the Falcons went home the victors of a tough conference fight. Sonam stayed for a good fifteen minutes after the final buzzer, cheering and celebrating with the rest of the students. It felt good to pull it out—even if it was a somewhat ugly experience in the process.

Overwrought Fans

The passion and enthusiasm of student fans during a home game are factors that make college sports so entertaining. Students commonly paint themselves in their school's colors, wear outlandish outfits, or create posters supporting their team. Furthermore, student fans are notorious for making noise during games. At a college football game, fans can create more than 110 decibels of sound. Crowd noise can be a significant factor in a game as it can disrupt the focus and communication of the opposing team.

In recent years, student fans have added a few new disruption tools to their repertoire with the help of Google and social networking sites. One new disruption tool popular with student fans is to scavenge the Internet for embarrassing information about individual players on the opposing team and then incorporate it into chants and signs during games.

For example, in a 2008 basketball game between the University of Memphis and the University of Alabama, Birmingham, an Alabama student made a sign reading "we beat Memphis not our girls" in reference to a complaint filed against a Memphis player for allegedly striking his girlfriend at a nightclub.[22] Similar types of signs, chants, and jeers that focus on an individual player's personal life and conduct on or off the field of play have raised controversy across the country.[23]

Other fans have used social networking sites, such as Facebook and MySpace, to access personal information (i.e., phone number and email address) from unsuspecting athletes on opposing teams. Fans then inundate the player with harassing calls, texts, and messages.[24]

Another trend for some student fans is to use profane chants. Student fans of West Virginia University's men's basketball team made national headlines when the Mountaineer Maniacs, a student group that attends home basketball games, led fans in chants such as "F- - - the Buckeyes" and "Eat s - - - Pitt." The chants were so loud, they could be heard on national television.[25] Similarly, students at the University of Kansas chant "Rip his f - - - ing head off" when their Jayhawks kick off to opposing teams.[26] This chant was adopted from the Adam Sandler movie *The Waterboy* and has become a tradition at the school.

The overwhelming majority of student fans behave responsibly during games; however, for some fans, the line between cheering for their team and engaging in uncivil conduct has become blurred. Fans cheer, jeer, and make noise to give their team a competitive advantage, but at what point does the fan enthusiasm go too far?

Sonam's experience at the basketball game caused her to confront the confusion that some students experience between passionately supporting their team and condoning uncivil conduct. What may appear to be harmless fun, like circulating an opposing player's phone number found on Facebook, can drastically disrupt the affected player's life. Imagine being inundated with calls and messages from fans wanting to talk trash.[27]

When the crowd chanted "rapist" as an opposing player was introduced, the intent was clearly to get into the player's head and make him lose focus. However, such chants, particularly when the evidence supporting it is sketchy, hit below the belt and are inappropriate at best. Most athletes recognize that opposing fans will yell derogatory and provocative statements from the stands. However, when a player's personal life is pushed into the game, things like struggles with drugs, past relationships, or sexual orientation, one has to wonder whether fan support has not turned into fan abuse.

Coordinated obscenities chanted by fans raise questions about the appropriateness of fan cheering and civility. While college games are usually attended by students and adults, college games are also attended by families with young children. Often games are televised and broadcasted on national television and cable. When fans use vulgar language during a game, they disregard others in the audience who may be offended by such banter, as well as the possibility that their conduct could create a barrier for their team from being broadcast on television and cable, which could have significant financial repercussions.[28]

POSTGAME FAN VIOLENCE

Jacob

Walking home from the football game, Jacob could never remember feeling so dejected in his life. *We had it,* he thought. *If we had just held on for the last forty-five seconds.* He stared at the sidewalk as he wandered back to the dorms.

A sudden *bam* caught his attention. He turned and looked around the corner of Wilson Hall, a building near the middle of campus. Six young men—all dressed in body paint and smelling strongly of alcohol—were tugging over a Dumpster tucked behind the building and slinging the trash all over the place.

Jacob knew better than to interfere. He walked on toward the main street that ran alongside the main part of campus.

He would have been forgiven for mistaking it for a war zone. Flashing red and blue lights lit the ghostly empty street. Three cars were on their sides, with one showing an obvious attempt to scratch expletives on its passenger side door. Two trash cans were on fire, and another one rolled on its side, charred from flames.

At the end of the street, police and paramedics had surrounded the intersection. Two girls lay in the street with jackets propping up their heads. A car with a bent bumper and cracked windshield sat abandoned in the middle lane—the obvious cause of the destruction. A small crowd of students surrounded the scene, gaping as police officers handcuffed and questioned the dazed driver.

As bad as he felt, Jacob simply couldn't help being awed by the scene. *Who does that? Who would trash a campus and risk lives over something this stupid?*

Then a thought stuck him.

Another time, could it have been me?

Who Does These Things?

It is difficult to explain logically why students would want to rip out goal posts and seats, start fires and vandalize, or assault and injure others following a big win or loss. It really does not make sense. Nevertheless, college fans have been known to riot after big games. The end result of such out-of-control fan revelry can be devastating. Student fans often face criminal charges as well as expulsion from school, people are needlessly injured, and property damage costs can reach hundreds of thousands of dollars.[29]

Research suggests that communities hosting Division I-A college football games experience sharp increases in assaults, vandalism, and arrests for disorderly conduct and alcohol-related offenses on game days.[30] When an upset loss occurs, the expected level of assaults and vandalism increases even more significantly.[31]

However, the spike in student misconduct is not just a college football phenomenon. In 2010, police broke up a rowdy student celebration at the University of Maryland after the men's basketball team defeated rival Duke. According to the police, a group tried to flip a bus, set trash cans on fire, and ripped off street signs.

In 2003, fans from both the winning and the losing teams of the NCAA hockey championship turned violent in two separate outbreaks.[32] Immediately following the championship game, fans of the winning University of Minnesota hit the streets of Minneapolis and began to break windows of shop owners, set vehicles ablaze, and throw rocks and chunks of concrete at emergency workers. Likewise, about four thousand fans of losing University of New Hampshire went to the streets in downtown Durham. It took more than two hours for police to get the crowd under control.

What causes students to react in violence to the outcome of an athletic competition? Andy Geiger, Ohio State's athletic director, told the *Chronicle of Higher Education* that "colleges encourage fans to be obnoxious to visiting teams by seating students at courtside, putting pep bands behind visitors' bleachers, [and] playing and replaying questionable referees' calls on video screens."[33] These factors may contribute to deteriorating fan behavior. When a team loses, particularly in an upset, spectator aggression may be caused by the shock that occurs when a dedicated fan's team loses a game. Aggressive behavior may naturally progress after a loss and may be viewed as "an attempt to recoup self-esteem."[34]

Jacob experienced the devastation that can occur when students react with violence after a loss. He asks himself a very poignant question—*Who would trash a campus and risk lives over something this stupid?*

5

Three things in human life are important: The first is to be kind. The second is to be kind, and the third is to be kind.

—**Henry James**

RESIDENTIAL LIFE

According to a 2008 federal census estimate, 2.3 million students now live in university housing.[1] Of that figure, 96 percent, or more than 2.2 million, are between the ages of eighteen and twenty-four, with a median age of nineteen and a half. By any measure, there are a huge number of young adults living in close quarters with one another on the modern college campus. And according to official sources, demand for college housing is still on the rise.[2]

The social dynamics between college roommates, especially freshman students, can be very challenging. Although many institutions have systems for matching roommates based on certain commonalities, roommates are usually complete strangers. Students and their parents may be anxious about compatibility: everything from cleanliness habits and preference in television programs to attitudes about alcohol and sexual orientation. Students now use social networks to look up personal information about their roommates before arriving on campus and may request reassignments before they move in.[3]

Although few freshman students request roommate changes during their freshman years, most will likely encounter conflict involving civility issues.[4] This chapter will assess some of the civility issues that roommates may experience in the context of on-campus student housing. As is inevitable with communal living at any age, several civility issues arise out of student housing. Ranging from the ones that instantly come to mind— roommate disputes over cleaning habits and noise levels—to ones that may seem conceptually foreign to a discussion on civil behavior—like illegally copying and sharing digital media—these issues confront college students every day literally in the place where many of them live. Before beginning the discussion on civility, let's briefly examine how the current college and university residential system evolved.

HISTORY OF COLLEGE DORMITORIES

The history of college dormitories extends back to the fourteenth century when the University of Bologna, University of Paris, and Oxford University all built residences for their students on campus.[5] These residences were only places to live; the schools did not monitor students' behavior.

Over the next few centuries, European universities evolved in two different directions on residence halls. Oxford first allowed the students to elect leaders of its halls but eventually came to assume complete control over their governance by appointing presiding faculty members. The continental schools, on the other hand, slowly backed away from providing any sort of school-sponsored living arrangements.[6]

When the colonists in America formed their own academic institutions, they modeled them after the familiar ones they knew in England. Thus, the American college system adopted a model of providing university housing for students while maintaining strict control over students' conduct. In effect, this was simply another form of *in loco parentis*, as discussed in chapter 1, where the schools assumed the roles of the students' parents.[7]

This model remained fairly static until the nineteenth and twentieth centuries. As the notion of *in loco parentis* broke down, so did the intellectual support for a model of university control over students' living arrangements. Today, residence life poses a difficult question: How to reconcile and balance two very conflicting visions of the institution's role in students' daily lives?

One thing that is certain is that the amenities of modern campus housing are much better than they were in the past. Long gone are the days of students going without heating and having to break the ice on water basins in order to get through cold winters.[8] In the second half of the twentieth century, student housing went from bare cinderblock walls with communal bathrooms to modern suite-style residences, with shared common areas and kitchens.[9] The demand for modern student housing is increasing.[10] Administrators anticipate the dormitories of the future to be modular and modern, with each room having its own bathroom.[11]

UNCIVIL ROOMMATES

No matter how well the students are housed, problems arise anytime multiple people share a small space. Scholars who have conducted extensive research on the personal conflict issues inherent in modern residence life propose numerous ideas for responding to conflicts.[12] Universities have tuned in to the problems, going to great lengths in their roommate-matching programs designed to produce the fewest number of conflicts possible.[13]

The basic problem with roommate living arrangements goes back to a familiar theme: a lack of civility. Treating others with a lack of respect in any way that violates the Golden Rule is a huge problem in residence life, where students are constantly in close contact with one another.

Lindsey

Lindsey slammed the door of the minifridge in frustration. She had suspected that she was slowly losing her Diet Dr. Peppers, but now she had concrete proof. She had carefully counted four of them left in there as of yesterday afternoon, but when she went to grab one today, only three were left.

I hate how she does that! she thought. *I don't want to be all territorial about my stuff, but it's clear that sharing a fridge is how she survives.*

Life with Megan had been anything but easy. Even though she and Lindsey had been good friends in high school, they quickly realized that hanging out on the weekends was fundamentally different from sharing the same room. It wasn't long before the girls discovered that they shared almost none of the most basic habits. While Lindsey was an early riser—preferring the relative calm of 7:00 a.m. for catching up on homework—Megan rarely saw the sunrise unless she was about to head to bed. Megan had also gone all out in the classic girlie dorm room deco, with pink and green everywhere, bulletin boards on the wall, and movie posters from home; Lindsey wasn't ever asked, but she preferred something a little simpler since they had to sleep in the room. Neither girl was a complete neat freak, but each had her own tics. Lindsey couldn't use a dirty bathroom, but didn't care too much about making her bed or having a few unfolded clothes lying draped across her computer chair. Megan, on the other hand, couldn't stand too much clutter in the "living space," but never saw cleaning the bathroom as worth more than about ten minutes of effort.

Nonetheless, the girls had managed so far to put a smile on it and stick it out, keeping their frustration (mostly) politely contained. They had decided to fend for themselves on food and other essentials—even toilet paper, noting their suite mates' propensity to forget to buy it when it was their turn—thus avoiding unnecessary conflicts. They had a couple of conversations about proper hours for visitors—Megan wasn't as worried about the dorm rule that visitors needed to be out by 1:00 a.m.—but nothing major.

But this is it! Lindsey thought. *Time to do something.* She pulled out a large sticky note pad and wrote a short, awkward message.

When Megan walked in from her 11:00 class, she found the note posted to the door. She peeled it off and read it:

> Hey, Meg,
>
> We're running low on DDP. Please leave the rest of them in there unless you want to go buy some more.
>
> Thanks!
>
> Linz

Seriously? Megan wondered. Lindsey had been getting irritable lately, but now she had lost it. Megan hadn't touched the drinks in the fridge—she didn't even like diet soda. And now to be accused of taking it was ridiculous.

Megan stormed into the room, threw down her backpack, and stuck the note in the middle of her computer desk. Her mind raced through all the things that she could say in reply. In the last week, Lindsey had dumped her clothes all over the floor—about the same time that Megan wanted to have company over—and awakened her twice in the morning by g-chatting and issuing smothered laughs from the computer. And to make it worse, she was always bringing Ryan to hang out here in the evenings. Megan liked Ryan well enough, but it sure made the small room even more crowded.

Cracking open her laptop, Megan opened up an email and began to lay out her entire case against Lindsey. She left the "To" line blank, debating about the recipient—Lindsey herself or, the safer option, one of the residential advisers or even Megan's mom. At the very least she needed a sympathetic voice to know just how bad she had it.

As Megan got to the second sentence of the email, where she began to talk about the pettiness of a false accusation of stealing food, she started to feel a bit more contemplative. Looking at what she had written so far, it was clear that the email would turn a small fight over a soda into something much bigger. *Is it time for that? Should we get it all on the table?* she wondered.

Confronting Uncivil Roommates

In healthy roommate relationships there must be mutual respect for each other's' property, space, and preferences—everything from the decor of common areas to visiting hours. While roommates are usually willing to give each other a certain level of slack, the continual failure to demonstrate respect in the relationship could eventually lead to conflict. In a few cases conflict between roommates has escalated to violence and even death.[14]

Clearly, killing a roommate over an allegedly stolen soda would be absurd; nevertheless, it was interesting to see how both Lindsey and Megan had created long mental lists of each other's offending conduct. The slack they had given each other had apparently reached capacity. The Diet Dr. Pepper issue seemed to be the proverbial straw that broke the camel's back.

When a roommate's conduct becomes so offensive that it begins to negatively affect the relationship, it is probably time to talk. Ignoring significant problems is not an effective conflict resolution strategy. Avoiding the problem will most likely increase stress and further strain the relationship. In fact, roommate-related stress has been associated with decreases in student academic performance.[15] Moreover, ignoring the problem essentially gives the offending roommate permission to continue the misconduct.[16] If the problem is not communicated, the offending roommate will never know the behavior is creating a problem. Furthermore, if conflict continues without resolution, roommates may require new living arrangements, which can be inconvenient and expensive.

Lindsey's note to Megan was a good first step toward resolving the conflict. However, the accusatory tone of the note may have escalated the problem. Accusatory statements typically cause people to respond defensively, especially if the accusations are incorrect. This is precisely how Megan initially responded. As it turned out, Megan was not the soda bandit. Confronting relational problems, such as the ones that Lindsey and Megan encountered, can be awkward, but it is essential to establishing healthy relationships.

INCIVILITY IN THE DORM ROOM

Even when the problems do not involve relationships between roommates, dorm culture can bring trouble from a civility perspective. Residence life is the key place where student culture manifests. The modern college student watches over ten hours of television a week with the favorite show being Fox's *Family Guy*[17]—a cartoon notorious for its crude jokes about every sensitive topic imaginable, from religion to disabilities. Music of all genres worshipping a culture of sex, excess, alcohol, and violence fills many students' iPods. Pornography appears on computers hooked up to dorm Internet networks on a constant basis. Indeed, statistics show that between 70 and 80 percent of college-age men access pornography online in a given month.[18]

With the vast array of edgy entertainment options popular with students, there are many opportunities to unintentionally create a dorm room environment that could be offensive to a roommate. Even if the environment is not offensive to roommates, it may be offensive to guests. Attempting to prevent offending guests may seem outside the scope of reasonableness; after all, if guests are offended by the environment of another's dorm room, they can just leave. However, being mindful of guests does have advantages, as Antonio learned.

Antonio

Antonio had been dreading the conversation for the last two days. But he couldn't put it off.

"Hey, Zach."

His roommate didn't even look up from the video game he was playing.

"What?"

"Um… Nicole's coming over tonight, and…"

"What, the girl from the party last week? Sweet. Who else is coming?"

Antonio grinned. He always liked being the one with connections.

"Two of her friends, actually. I think we're going to watch *Lost* and then go out later. They're really into it… and they're hot."

"Mind if I tag along?" asked Zach.

"Sure—glad to share the wealth." Antonio hesitated. "There is one thing, though…"

I didn't want to have to do this, he thought. The issue had been bugging him for a week now, but he had put off bringing it up. "Would you mind helping me clean up the place?"

Zach laughed. "You worried about some chick being grossed out by our bathroom? Sure, I can do that."

Antonio smiled. But that wasn't what he meant.

A week ago, he had invited Amy—a girl from econ class—over to review some of the homework. While they were sitting at his desk going over stuff, he couldn't help noticing that she kept shifting uncomfortably in the room. For a while, he couldn't figure it out. He and Zach actually did a decent job of keeping things tolerably clean and odor-free—although there was only so much you could do to block out the scent wafting down the hallway of the frat house. But Amy seemed nervous nonetheless.

After working through one particularly complex marginal cost question, Antonio looked up in time to catch Amy staring at one of the walls. He followed her gaze and quickly pieced together her source of discomfort.

Up on the wall, tacked with putty, was a picture of a blonde in a bikini, staring lustily at the camera. Well, she was sort of in a bikini—at least the bottom part of one. The top half was in her hands, which she held against her breasts.

It had never occurred to Antonio that the poster—or the half dozen others like it scattered across the room—would make anyone feel uncomfortable. When Zach had pulled them out in the first place, he had admired them appreciatively, although secretly screening for any outright nudity—nipples, etc. Seeing that there was none, he decided that it was safe to put it up. Sure, his mom wouldn't be crazy about it, but he couldn't see how it violated any sort of rules.

But this was different. On seeing Amy's winced expression, he could feel his face start to redden. At that point, what could he do? Saying something would come off sounding either like a wussy ("Aw, those dumb posters my roommate put up") or downright boorish ("She's kind of hot, isn't she?"). He simply looked down at the page and made some comment—he couldn't even remember what—to get Amy's thoughts back to microeconomics.

Now, facing the prospect of spending an entire evening with three girls he liked to hang out with, he really didn't want it to happen again. *They might not care…* he had tried to convince himself unsuccessfully. The more he thought about it, the more he thought it was kind of weird.

"The bathroom's fine. Nicole's not picky about that. But what about out here? Think we can work on the main space?"

Maybe he'll figure out what I'm getting at. If not, this could get really awkward. Antonio had dreaded the possible—and to his mind, likely— end of the confrontation. Although the details were a little fuzzy, he was pretty sure it involved the *f* word and some comments about his sexual preferences.

"What do you mean?" Zach asked. The video game was now on pause. He looked around and, catching Antonio's gaze, just shrugged. "Do whatever the hell you want. Just put it back when you're done."

A Hostile Environment

Pornography ranges from mild to obscene; however, the distinctions are often blurry. For many the difference is based on how much skin is revealed. This was Zach's approach. He had made sure that the more than half dozen pictures that adorned his dorm room did not have any "outright nudity."

Interestingly, Zach's approach is fairly consistent with current law. The U.S. Supreme Court has defined obscene pornographic material as portraying "sexual conduct in a patently offensive way" or a way that "lacks serious literary, artistic, political, or scientific value."[19] The Supreme Court has also found that obscene material must appeal to something other than "normal, healthy sexual desires."[20] Most pornographic material does not fall under the U.S. Supreme Court's broad definition of obscene, unless for example, it involves children, violence, or sex with animals.[21] Nevertheless, erotic pictures, such as the ones in Antonio and Zach's room, would most likely be offensive to female students since the images depicted women as sexual objects. Clearly, Antonio's friend Amy was disturbed by the images.

Many colleges and universities develop policies that restrict access to erotic and pornographic material in public places, such as libraries and computer labs.[22] They have such policies because courts have found that the display of pornography in public areas can create a hostile environment, which is a form of gender discrimination.

While there is no federal law requiring students to eliminate a hostile environment in a private dorm room, there may be policies at the institutions that restrict certain types of images from being displayed in residence halls. However, even if there were no policies to restrict erotic and pornographic material in a dorm or apartment, a more civil approach would be for students to consider the effect of their décor on others.

VIRTUAL VIOLENCE

Violent video games are wildly popular with college students—especially guys.[23] With the constant improvement in video game graphics and technology, the level of detail incorporated into many violent video games can be very disturbing. While experts argue about the effects of video game violence on individuals, there may be broader civility issues associated with these games. For example, is the game offensive to another roommate, does it create a hostile environment for guests, and was it obtained legally?

Jacob

"Don't do that!"

"Gotcha."

"Gah!"

Jacob laughed. It was just another night of video games with Mark. There wasn't anything better than digitally shooting good friends after a dinner of chicken fingers and fries.

It was just another typical night of playing video games and hanging out together. Mark and Jacob hit it off immediately. Paired through the university's roommate-matching system, they soon found common interests (biking, video games) and common classes (they were both engineering majors). By October, they were already hitting up the same parties with the same crew and spending most other nights chilling at the dorm.

Mark wasn't from the area, but otherwise his story was a lot like Jacob's. He had grown up in a large town with a big circle of friends. But he wanted to branch out a bit and really make the most of his college years, so he took off across the country for school. Landing in the dorms a week before class started, he literally did not know a soul in the town. The thought hadn't fazed him, though—within a few weeks, he had gathered a circle of close friends from class and other campus activities.

"Hey, have you seen this yet?" Mark asked. He was now playing a single-player campaign in the game since Jacob had gotten up to check the fridge for any leftover chicken.

Jacob looked over and saw the familiar scene of a combat video game they had played before. He hadn't been through the single-player campaign, so he watched as Mark took over the control of the player.

The game was a first-person shooter, where the gamer took the role of a soldier and saw the screen from his perspective, giant automatic weapon in hand. This particular level was set at an airport. Jacob watched as Mark's player—an American soldier hidden as a double agent in a terrorist group—went up the elevator with a group of terrorists.

When the door opened, the group walked into a crowded airport. The state-of-the-art graphics rendering system made the crowded lines at the metal detectors very realistic, and Jacob could relate to the concept of standing in line.

But not to what happened next. At the signal of one computer character, Mark and the video game terrorists burst into fire, shooting into the airport crowd, lobbing grenades at them, and generally creating every type of havoc imaginable. Blood splattered on walls, benches, luggage, and other realistic props in the game. Unarmed civilians screamed and ran in terror; the wounded writhed on the ground in agony. Others attempted to drag away injured friends.

The terrorists—aided by Mark—would have none of it. They mercilessly shot at everything that moved, killing them in graphic fashion.

"What do you think?" Mark asked. There was a weird tone to his voice. "Pretty crazy, huh?"

Jacob hesitated. People had whined over the violence of video games for decades, but it never registered with him. *It's just a game, right? None of it's real.*

Still this seemed different. He couldn't remember another game where the breakdown of the good and the bad got so twisted up. Here, the "hero" was creating the most awful carnage imaginable for a group of innocent civilians. For once, he wished the lifelike realism of the gaming platform wasn't quite so good.

A few minutes later, there was a knock on the door. Jacob hopped up and opened it to find Jason, who lived two rooms down the hall.

"Hey, guys, check this out." Jason walked in holding a blank DVD.

"What?"

"The new *Bravo Squad*. Beta version, actually. We just got done downloading it."

Jacob looked at him hard. "You mean *Bravo 2*? I thought it wasn't coming out for another month or two."

Jason laughed. "Ha-ha, it's out already—you just have to know where to look. Come on. Go ahead and try it out on the LAN network. Don't get on the big world yet, though—the beta testers have been hunting down code hacks and blocking IPs."

That's a sixty-dollar game, Jacob thought. He didn't know whether to be impressed or concerned.

PIRATES OF THE DORMITORY

One of the newest incarnations of uncivil conduct in dorms might belong solely to the younger generations. Today's residence halls are hot spots for illegal downloads and piracy of movies and music. Students seem to lose the concept of ownership when it's made into an abstract principle and the owner doesn't have a tangible face. While the correlation between illegal downloading and civility may seem scant, there is an intersection. Illegal downloading is essentially a form of stealing, and stealing is an act that shows disregard for other people's property. This type of behavior can have significant negative effects for the person who was the victim of theft as well as the community.

Although colleges and universities have taken steps to curb illegal downloading, the practice persists.[24] Students who continue to engage in the practice will likely encounter disciplinary action by their school or in some cases face legal actions from the copyright owner.

Sonam

Residence life had suited Sonam just fine. She had enjoyed getting to know her roommate, Joanna, and their two suite mates, and they all had managed to stay out of each other's way just enough to avoid grinding on anyone's nerves. Each of them had her own circles of friends and really only spent time together a couple of nights a week.

Sonam had taken to getting the mail for the room every day. The mailbox was on her way back from the gym, so she didn't mind stopping by in the afternoon and picking it up. There wasn't usually much—maybe a care package from home about once a month, frequent credit card offers, and occasional magazines.

Today was different, though. When she stuck her hand in the mailbox, she pulled out an ivory-colored, official-looking envelope addressed to Joanna. *Weird*, she thought. But since they generally tried to stay out of each other's business, Sonam didn't give it any more thought after she placed it on Joanna's desk.

But there sure was some more thought on it that night. It happened to be a rare occasion when both girls were in for the evening at the same time. Joanna dumped out the stuff she had accumulated in her backpack throughout the day. Spying the letter, she grabbed it. "What's this?" she asked.

"No idea. Just grabbed it out of our mailbox today."

Joanna slid her finger into the adhered tab and ripped the envelope open. Inside, there was a letter printed on matching ivory stationery:

Dear Ms. Kelley,

We have asked your Internet Service Provider to forward this letter to you in advance of our filing a lawsuit against you in federal court for copyright infringement. We represent a number of large record companies, including SONY BMG MUSIC ENTERTAINMENT, Universal Music Group, and Warner Music Group, as well as all of their subsidiaries ("Record Companies") in pursuing claims of copyright infringement against individuals who have illegally uploaded or downloaded sound on peer-to-peer networks.

We have gathered evidence that you have been infringing copyrights owned by the Record Companies. We are attaching to this letter a sample of the sound recordings you were found distributing via the AresWarezUS (Ares) peer-to-peer network. In total, you were found to be distributing 321 files, a substantial number of which are sound recordings controlled by the Record Companies.

The reason we are sending this letter to you in advance of filing suit is to give you the opportunity to settle these claims as early as possible. If you contact us within the next twenty (20) calendar days, we will offer to settle the claims for a significantly reduced amount compared to the judgment amount a court may enter against you. **If we do not hear from you within 20 calendar days of your receipt of this letter, we will file suit against you in federal court.**

We are not your lawyers, and we will not provide you with any legal advice. Please consult an attorney if you have questions about your legal options.

Sincerely,

Robert Smith

"Oh, my God!" Joanna shouted. "This is ridiculous!" She silently reread the letter, her face slowly turning pinker than normal.

By now, Sonam had pieced it all together. Some of the people in her classes had gotten similar letters in the past week, threatening them with prosecution for illegal file sharing. But she never dreamed that it would happen to someone like Joanna. After all, all she did was download a bunch of Beyoncé and Taylor Swift songs she hadn't brought on CD from home. Surely that wasn't illegal. And besides, there were tons of guys even in their dorm who bragged about their extensive collection of movies they had downloaded online. Wasn't that even worse?

Sonam herself wasn't too worried. She had conflicting feelings about digital music sharing. Because she had several friends struggling to get signed with a recording label—although these proverbial starving artists generally lived with their families—she had given up downloading music a few years ago. But she had made that as a personal choice. She had no idea that the industry was starting to fight back. And it sure picked an easy target.

Illegal Downloads

Technology is everywhere on college campuses. Students have the opportunity to use technology almost constantly—from the laptops that they bring to class to type notes to their smart phones that provide instant access to the Internet and contain thousands of digitally downloaded songs. While the advances in technology offer new and exciting opportunities for both learning and entertainment, there are legal consequences for technology misuse.

One of the biggest misuses of technology at college campuses is illegal downloading of copyrighted music, movies, and video games through peer-to-peer networks. Peer-to-peer networks are systems that allow users to share information directly with other network users without accessing a central computer. In other words network users are able to access shared information directly from other network users' computers through the Internet. With the expansion of high-speed Internet connections on college campuses, peer-to-peer networks gained notoriety due to their ability to allow students to quickly and easily share copyrighted music and movies.

For years, preventing unauthorized downloading of copyrighted digital media was mired in confusion over the legality of the practice and the attitudes and perceptions of many students that the practice was "sharing," not "stealing." In 2005, the U.S. Supreme Court helped clear up much of the confusion regarding the legality of sharing copyrighted material over peer-to-peer networks.[25] The Supreme Court found that Grokster, the owner of popular peer-to-peer file-sharing software, had intentionally induced copyright infringement and could be held liable for the acts of its users. This ruling was a landmark decision because the Grokster software did not actually violate copyright laws—instead it facilitated infringement. Nevertheless, the Court found that Grokster was more than just an innocent bystander to the infringement occurring on its network. There was sufficient evidence to demonstrate that the company actually encouraged users to violate copyright laws.[26]

In response to the U.S. Supreme Court's decision in *Grokster*, the music and movie industries brought suit against both peer-to-peer network users (direct infringers) and the creators of networking software. The Recording Industry Association of America and the Motion Picture Association of America filed hundreds of "John Doe" lawsuits against the most active illegal downloaders at eighteen colleges. These trade associations identified the unnamed student defendants by their computer's IP addresses.[27]

In 2007 the Recording Industry Association of America implemented a new strategy in an attempt to deter piracy. Similar to the lawsuits it previously filed, it identified student infringers based on their computers' IP addresses. However, once a student was identified, the association sent the accused student a pre-litigation letter instead of one declaring a lawsuit. The goal of this new approach was to offer students an opportunity to settle claims before they turned into lawsuits of public record.

Sonam's roommate was one of the students who received a pre-litigation letter from the Recording Industry Association of America. The initial response was shock and disbelief for both Sonam and her roommate. Interestingly, the music that Joanna had illegally downloaded was apparently music she had previously purchased. It appeared that Joanna believed she was entitled to the downloaded music, even if she did not pay for it, because she had the albums at home.

Sonam's response to the situation was also interesting. She believed that the morality of file sharing is a personal choice. Implied in this belief is that taking copyrighted music without authorization or payment is not intrinsically wrong. However, in many ways illegally downloading music, movies, and other protected media is akin to shoplifting or plagiarizing a research paper. It is taking something without permission.

Piracy harms more than just affluent superstars and large record labels. According to the Institute for Policy Innovation, global piracy has resulted in more than 71,000 lost jobs, $2.7 billion in workers' lost earnings, and a loss of $422 million in tax revenues.[28] Furthermore, the loss in revenues caused by piracy undermines the future of music because it limits the resources available to record companies to develop new talent.[29]

Currently, the Recording Industry Association of America has stopped filing lawsuits against individuals. The association claims that it stopped suing individuals based on a stronger antipiracy initiative taken by leading Internet service providers and the new legal clarity on what types of information can be shared on peer-to-peer networks.[30] Since the lawsuits have ended, the association claims there has been greater awareness of the illegality of downloading without permission and significant growth in the revenues earned from legal online marketplaces.[31] Nevertheless, there are still plenty of illegal peer-to-peer file-sharing networks that continue to provide access to protected media for free and without permission.

6

*One of the things I learned when I was
negotiating was that until I changed
myself, I could not change others.*
—**Nelson Mandela, April 2000**

THE QUESTION OF HEALTHY BEHAVIORS

So far, we've concentrated on issues of civility that deal with students and how they interact with others. But there's another side of civility that needs to be taken into account. When students act in ways that harm or otherwise degrade *themselves*, those actions have civility implications. The clearest example is the classic case of drunk driving, where the driver makes the self-destructive choice to consume too much alcohol and then drives and causes a serious wreck, hurting someone else. Those situations are easy to classify as uncivil because they show a manifest disregard for one's own safety and the safety of others.

Self-destructive harmful behavior may also be uncivil because it undermines cultural norms and standards established to promote civil behaviors. For example, engaging in a heavy drinking may not directly harm anyone, but it might just contribute to a general acceptance of such behavior as a campus norm and thus encourage others to engage in similar actions. Even simple peer pressure might come into play in prompting others to mirror unhealthy activities.

Finally, self-destructive behaviors may also create negative consequences for others, especially for family and friends. When students harm themselves as a result of high-risk conduct, their family and friends may experience a gamut of emotions ranging from severe concern to guilt, especially when students are injured as a result of their behavior. To the extent that the behavior creates unnecessary stress for others, it, too, has civility implications.[1]

The concept of civility encompasses behaviors that traditionally might be viewed as personal. However, personal behavior can affect a community. Because of this, many behavioral issues currently facing college students fit in well with a discussion on civility in general. In this chapter, we discuss how student behaviors on the college campus contribute to civility and incivility.

DRINKING AND SUBSTANCE ABUSE

Students at many colleges and universities seem to embrace a culture of drinking and partying. Alcohol and drugs are readily available, and peers celebrate and encourage self-destructive behavior. The pressure for new students to accept the party culture as the norm is intense, especially when it appears that everyone else on campus is living "la vida loca" and having fun. Partying may be part of the college experience; however, it can get out of control, as Antonio discovered.

Antonio

Antonio glared out of the corner of his eye at Dan, whose head was thrown back too far to see him. This was the fourth time someone had knocked over the stack of cards in the middle, initiating the "waterfall," where each person playing the game had to chug his beer for as long as the person in front of him was drinking. Dan was both heavy and a heavy drinker, and he had no qualms about chugging away at Antonio's expense. It was only Thursday night, and Antonio hadn't intended to get anything more than a buzz. This game posed a threat to that plan.

In fact, this was the third night out of the last six that Antonio was drinking. He hadn't planned it that way, and he had only a couple of beers on two of those evenings, but he did realize that it was starting to be more of a habit than a periodic indulgence. That was the price of hanging out with the fraternity brothers. Alcohol accompanied everything they did together—from meetings to video games to intramural athletics to actual parties. It simply was a part of their lifestyle.

What bothered Antonio wasn't the drinking itself but the extent of it. He never minded a buzzed party where everyone was just a little relaxed, easy to talk to. The jokes were funnier, the music was better, and everyone had a better time. But what got to him was the extent of the heavy drinking. After a few mornings of puking up his guts from a night of drinking games or other excesses, he quickly determined that he wasn't a Bluto Blutarsky by any means.

The problem was that his fraternity brothers were—and demanded that he play along. He knew of several members who managed to drink more than eight beers at a time on more than three or four nights in a given week. But unlike Antonio, the real drinkers had managed to prune down their other obligations in order to focus on feeding the alcohol habit. Antonio, on the other hand, kept going to classes every morning, going to baseball workouts in the afternoon, and managing to squeeze in time with nonfraternity friends. The morning headaches and exhaustion really messed up his routine.

By about eleven o'clock that evening, the party was in a lull between the initial round of pregaming and the real start to the festivities around midnight when everyone else and the rented band would arrive. Despite his buzz, Antonio realized that this was his chance to duck out and catch up on some much needed sleep upstairs in his room.

As he stepped off the stairs and into the hallway, he heard noise coming out of the open doorway to the left—his room. He stepped in and saw Ethan, an older, quiet brother, digging around in his dresser. Antonio quickly went rigid with agitation and confusion, but he decided to play it cool.

"Uh, hey, man. You need something?"

Ethan turned around and saw him, breaking into a wide grin. "Hey, bro, what's up?"

The two looked at each other for a second. Antonio decided to go into the obvious.

"Anything in particular you need in here?"

At the frat house, it wasn't odd at all to be in each other's space. Doors generally stayed open, and the brothers in the fraternity didn't have huge reservations about going in each other's rooms. But personal stuff—drawers and desks—was a different story.

Ethan grinned a bit. "Nope. Just putting some stuff away. You don't mind me keeping it here, do you?"

Antonio squinted a bit, confused. "Keeping what? What the hell are you talking about?"

Ethan laughed. "Calm down. It's no big deal. Look, I'll even give you a bit for the trouble."

At that moment, Antonio first noticed the little plastic baggie that Ethan had crumpled in his hand. It was filled with just a little bit of some sort of green-brown stuff. *You have got to be kidding me,* thought Antonio. *No way is that stuff staying in my room!*

He had heard for some time that there was a source somewhere in the frat for marijuana. It wasn't something the brothers came out and talked about, but no one was under any illusion about whether it was available for the interested. Antonio had even seen several of the brothers passing bongs or bowls after parties in the privacy of their own rooms. He figured it didn't really matter that much—*I mean, everyone smokes at least sometimes, right?*—but now he sure as hell didn't want it in his room.

He cleared his throat. "Look. That needs to go somewhere else. I'm not your dope-boy."

Ethan's smile faded, and he straightened up. He spoke quietly and seriously: "Look. I asked nicely the first time. Now I'm giving you an order. You don't have to touch it, don't have to use, don't have to buy it—but those bags are staying in those drawers. And good luck telling Michael or anyone else—I'll let you guess who they'll side with." Ethan shoved past Antonio and stormed into the hallway.

Now what? Breathing heavily, Antonio looked around. He wasn't sure if he was furious, scared, confused, or some combination of all three. He had given a second's thought to making a fight out of it with Ethan, but the beer on his brain had made him just slow enough not to respond right away. Now, he didn't know what to do. *Michael's in on it, too?* Michael was the frat president, who generally seemed to be on top of things. Short of going to the administration or police—which would be suicide for his membership—he didn't see many options.

Maybe I'm just being too uptight about all this, he thought. He had tried marijuana once in high school, got a weird feeling out of it, and generally avoided it since. Now with the threat of ramifications from baseball weighing in, he felt the risks of having anything patently illegal in his system outweighed the benefit of a new high. But he knew that others in his frat—and in the student body as a whole—viewed marijuana use as no big deal. Maybe it wasn't worth all the stress.

Alcohol Abuse

According to the National Institute on Alcohol Abuse and Alcoholism, student misuse of alcohol is the "most important health hazard for college students."[2] Binge drinking, the practice of consuming five or more drinks on a single occasion (sometimes adjusted to four or more drinks for women), has been associated with a number of adverse consequences.[3] Most students are aware that heavy drinking will likely result in a hangover, perhaps nausea, and even alcohol-induced memory loss. These risks seem rather benign and manageable. However, high-risk drinking among college students accounts for more than 599,000 unintentional injuries, 696,000 assaults, 97,000 sexual assaults, as well as 1,700 deaths every year.[4] Often those injured as a result of student alcohol abuse are innocent bystanders who happen to be in the wrong place at the wrong time. This is where binge drinking crosses the line from personal choice to an issue involving civility.

The data suggest that alcohol and drug abuse is a major problem for many colleges and universities. According to a study conducted by the National Center on Addiction and Substance Abuse (CASA), nearly half of America's full-time students use illicit drugs or binge drink at least once a month.[5] However, the risk of substance abuse among students varies statistically based on certain demographics and subgroups. For example, men generally tend to drink more than women.[6] In addition to gender, there is evidence to suggest race and ethnicity may be a risk factor. White students tend to be the heaviest drinkers, followed by Latino and then African-American and Asian students.[7]

Regardless of gender, race, or ethnicity, students who are at highest risk of alcohol and substance abuse are athletes and members of fraternities and sororities.[8] Students who are both athletes and members of a Greek organization have the highest rate of binge drinking on campus.[9]

Antonio is probably unaware that as an athlete and a member of a fraternity, he is in a high-risk subgroup of students for binge drinking. His experiences seem to confirm his status. According to Antonio, alcohol consumption was central to his fraternity's lifestyle. Drinking accompanied almost every activity at the house. While he enjoyed the occasional buzz, drinking—and drinking heavily—was becoming more habitual for him and the other members of the fraternity. Choosing not to engage in the drinking festivities did not seem to be an option as his fraternity brothers essentially demanded participation.

Antonio's experience illustrates an interesting quandary. Does involvement in Greek organizations per se foster more alcohol abuse, or alternatively, do new students who are already heavy drinkers seek membership in fraternities or sororities to facilitate existing drinking habits?[10] Clearly, Antonio had no qualms about drinking moderately; however, his friend Dan and others in the fraternity would drink as many as eight beers at one time three or four times a week. Despite Antonio's desire to keep his drinking manageable, the environment in the fraternity house seemed to encourage and directly contribute to his higher levels of alcohol consumption.

Researchers have speculated for years about why students in Greek organizations are more likely to engage in binge drinking. The reasons are complex; however, there is evidence to suggest that both social influences (i.e., peer pressure and an enabling environment) and student self-selection (i.e., intentionally associating with groups that drink heavily) can contribute to the higher rate of alcohol abuse in Greek organizations than in the general student population.[11] Given this environment, students who drink moderately are more likely to transition to binge drinking.

As discussed in chapter 2, it would be inaccurate to state that all fraternities and sororities support an environment of reckless alcohol abuse. Many Greek organizations have taken meaningful steps to combat the *Animal House* behavior and stigma. Moreover, there are Greek organizations deeply committed to intellectual enrichment of their members and community service. Although a vast body of research seems to confirm that members of Greek organizations remain among the heaviest drinkers on campus, abuse is not just a Greek issue. The pervasiveness of underage drinking is an issue that affects all students.

While some students may view heavy drinking as a personal choice that does not affect other people, this perception is not entirely accurate.

Alcohol abuse can impose uncivil consequences on others. Drunken students can become loud, violent, and argumentative, and they generally create problems. More sober friends may be required to essentially babysit the drunken students to make sure that they stay out of trouble. Taking care of a drunken friend may be annoying and may result in interrupted study or sleep time.

Substance Abuse

While not as pervasive as binge drinking, the use of illegal drugs, especially marijuana, is not uncommon at college parties and social events. Marijuana is the most popular illicit drug among college students. One study found that 47.5 percent of college students had tried marijuana in their lifetime and 16.8 percent had used marijuana in the past month.[12]

Interestingly, there is a strong correlation between students who binge drink and students who use illicit drugs.[13] Students who binge drink are substantially more likely to use marijuana than students who occasionally drink or those who do not drink.[14] Moreover, nearly all people who use marijuana also use alcohol.[15] Some research suggests that when colleges reduce rates of student alcohol abuse, drug use also declines.

Like binge drinking, frequent marijuana use is associated with a number of problems, ranging from poorer academic performance to increased rates of harmful social and behavioral problems.[16] Students who are high on marijuana are likely to exhibit some of the same behavior as intoxicated students, such as fighting, vandalism, and overall reckless behavior.[17] Marijuana use—which is illegal—is often referred to as a "gateway drug" because it introduces users to the illicit drug scene, which can lead users to experiment with other more dangerous drugs such as cocaine, heroin, and psychotherapeutic drugs.[18]

When Antonio confronted Ethan, he was shocked to find marijuana in his room. Possession of a controlled substance is a criminal offense in most areas. A conviction could affect his eligibility to play baseball, endanger his athletic scholarship, and be grounds for disciplinary sanctions from the school. Ethan, however, was unfazed by Antonio's demand or even the possible threat that Antonio might report him to the authorities. It appeared that tolerance for drugs had reached the highest levels of leadership in the house. Antonio seemed to have no easy options.

IMAGE CONSCIOUSNESS

Image-conscious students concerned about their weight tend to fall within a continuum. On one end of the continuum are students who are essentially indifferent. They may claim they want to lose weight, but lack motivation to initiate change. These students often continue to eat unhealthy, gain weight, and eventually become overweight or obese. On the other end are students who become so intent on weight loss that they skip meals or are constantly dieting or exercising. The students at this end of the continuum sometimes develop eating disorders.

Eating disorders are caused by a complex mix of psychological, biological, and environmental issues.[19] Social factors can trigger disorders. For example, negative comments about another person's weight and the glorification of thinness and the perfect body among peers can create an environment fostering unhealthy eating habits.

Lindsey

Despite their continuing friendship, Lindsey and her roommate, Megan, had taken dramatically different directions in school. Megan had hit college running, but not in the healthy sense. She dove headfirst into activities with her sorority and campus government, but didn't hit the gym with the same eagerness. Worse, her newly acquired taste for beer added calories to her life that weren't going away any time soon. She spent every morning sleeping in, every afternoon sitting in class, evenings lounging in front of the TV, and nights making the rounds at keggers.

Lindsey, on the other hand, had managed to stave off the infamous freshman fifteen, but it had been *hard* work. She had taken to skipping breakfast several mornings a week—which she thought wasn't much of a sacrifice since it afforded her an extra half hour of sleep—and religiously made it to the student recreation center in the afternoons for a forty-five-minute session on the elliptical trainer with some of her sorority sisters. *Thank God for that,* she thought. The exercise kept her in shape and made some of the stress more bearable.

For whatever reason, though, her mom had freaked out about it when Lindsey went home back in October. Claiming that she was as skinny as a rail, her mom had rehashed several tired lines—complete with statistics—about the prevalence of eating disorders among girls in college and the dangers of an inadequate diet. Lindsey knew better than to argue with her mom about it, but she couldn't help thinking that her mom was being ridiculous. After all, she hadn't really lost much weight since she started college, just a few pounds. And she definitely knew what eating disorders looked like. She could probably name half a dozen friends off the top of her head who more appropriately needed to listen to her mom's spiel.

But as she continued to feign attention, one fact did unsettle her a bit. Of those half dozen friends, nearly every one of them was in Lindsey's sorority. Come to think of it, she couldn't name a single girl in her sorority who she hadn't seen skip a meal every now or then or opt to "drink her dinner" and forgo food calories for those in light beer.

She could also remember some of the more damning comments that leaked out one night during a chapter meeting. The sorority had just had a rough run-in with campus administration when the members were the invited guests of one of the fraternities for a swap at the frat house. As it turned out, things had gotten out of hand, and the school had issued a formal reprimand to the fraternity for public disturbance, underage drinking, and some lewd acts by a few of its members. While Lindsey's sorority had managed to avoid the headlines and a formal rebuke, the president and a few of the other officers had been called before the Dean of Student Affairs for an intense meeting—although it sounded more like a dressing-down—about their behavior. That translated at the chapter's next meeting into angry leaders, who felt the time had come to air all the problems with the sisters and pledges.

The problem was that those problems weren't constrained to their unladylike conduct at the party. On top of lecturing them about the obvious sins—drinking straight out of beer bottles instead of pouring it into opaque plastic cups, openly flirting with the wrong frat guys, sleeping around too much—the sorority treasurer had other complaints that apparently had been tormenting her for a while. When it came around to her time to speak, she began with a stinging comment about how the pledge class was a bunch of "fat heifers that couldn't take care of themselves" and that the sorority was in danger of losing more than its reputation "if it gave the sense it was growing pigs and cattle."

Lindsey had winced a bit at the time, but looking back, it was painful. Every girl in the sorority was—by any objective standard—skinny, trim, and pretty, but each was also dreadfully self-conscious about body issues. Those comments had only added more fuel to that fire.

The Freshman Fifteen

It is relatively common for students to gain ten to fifteen pounds by the end of their freshman year. This weight gain, nicknamed "the freshman fifteen," is typically the result of two factors—a reduction in physical activity and an increase in caloric intake. Freshman students tend to be less physically active than they were in high school. Students who participated in high school sports and other extracurricular physical activities, such as dance, gymnastics, and karate, often do not continue these activities during their freshman year. The motivation to exercise can take a backseat to adjusting to college life and partying with friends.

In addition to the reduction in physical activity, it is easy to lapse into more casual, unhealthy eating habits. Students commonly miss breakfast, the most important meal of the day to get a person's metabolism moving. College cafeterias do not always offer healthy choices, and even if they do, new students may gravitate toward food with marginal nutritional value. The most popular meal order in a college cafeteria is chicken fingers, fries, and a carbonated beverage.[20] Students are prone to eat more late night snacks and consume large amounts of high-calorie alcoholic beverages.

Lindsey was very aware of the so-called freshman fifteen. Although her diet was not ideal, she made it a point to exercise regularly with other members of her sorority and keep in shape, even shedding a few pounds. While Lindsey was driven to stay fit and look her best, Megan did not have the same drive. Like many freshman students, Megan became very sedentary and began to gain weight.

When Lindsey returned home, she was quick to dismiss her mother's concerns, yet she remembered some scathing comments made by leaders in her sorority implying that pledges were fat. Perhaps these mean-spirited comments were subconsciously contributing to Lindsey's drive to stay fit and control her weight. Whether her mother's concerns are merited is unknown, but Lindsey, whether she realized it or not, was beginning to exhibit symptoms of an eating disorder. The sorority environment was not conducive to healthy attitudes about eating and weight.

Learning to live healthfully is an important skill for college students. Eating healthy, nutritious meals, limiting high-calorie foods, and getting regular exercise go a long way toward maintaining a healthy weight and long-term quality of life. While students may try to encourage their friends and acquaintances to take better care of themselves, brash and offensive comments about another's appearance are hurtful and the wrong type of encouragement.

DEPRESSION AND SUICIDE

The transition to college can be extremely stressful. Students may be anxious about leaving home, living on campus, and making new friends. Some have difficulties adjusting to the speed and demands of college-level courses or experience problems balancing their social lives with academic responsibilities. Others may feel extreme pressure to achieve and focus intensely on grades. Many are worried about the rising cost of education. These stressors are normal for college students.

While most students are able to handle these challenges, managing the stress of college along with other life stressors can become too much to handle for some students. Sometimes this out-of-control feeling is just a passing emotion; however, sometimes the feeling is the result of a biological illness known as depression. Students who suffer from depression are not able to function at their best. They often experience loss of interest in usual activities, fatigue, loss of energy, and a diminished ability to think or concentrate.[21] Depressed students are also at risk for suicide.

Sonam

Sonam had become intensely worried about her suite mate Tania. While they had initially struck it off quite well and tried out the same restaurants, classes, and campus events, Tania had gradually faded into living a very routine existence, which rarely drew her outside the walls of the dorm. She usually went to classes and might make a store run occasionally for refills on soda, frozen dinners, and bags of chips, but that was about the extent of her involvement with anything. Sonam had at first tried to pry her away for parties, for restaurant outings, for church—really, for just about anything—but Tania's inclination to decline had gradually worn down Sonam's energy to invite her. They now lived separate lives and only interacted in the few hours at night when Sonam returned to the dorm and ventured next door to say hi. Other than that, Tania limited her interaction with the outside world to only what was absolutely necessary.

Sonam couldn't help wondering just how much Courtney had to do with Tania's shift in behavior. Courtney was her ex-boyfriend who had chosen their reunion over winter break as the most convenient time to let Tania know that he had found out that college was a wonderful place to meet people and that he thought they needed to go their separate ways. Tania, on the other hand, had never imagined such a possibility and had spent much of the first semester considering the prospect of transferring schools to be with him. The breakup was unexpected and hard, and it definitely left its mark.

If it weren't for an email from the dorm's resident adviser, Sonam probably would have written off Tania's behavior. The university apparently had just decided to launch a Mental Health Awareness Day for all of its on-campus residents, and the residence life employees were sending out warning signs of depression and other illnesses. Sonam had heard that the inspiration for the efforts wasn't totally benign—the rumor was that a girl in one of the dorms across the quad had been found with alcohol and a stomach full of painkillers a few weeks ago. They got her to the hospital in time, and there were no serious consequences, but it definitely was a scary moment. No one was using the *s* word, but the school apparently figured that there was a good chance that was the case.

The hard part now was that the bottom of the RA's email included a plea for information about any residents in the hall who were exhibiting signs of withdrawal, fatigue, and mood changes—signs that fit Tania completely. Sonam didn't have any idea what to do. Tania was her friend, and Sonam had no doubt that referring her to residence life for a mental health evaluation wouldn't do wonders for their friendship. Tania probably wouldn't take all that kindly to the invasion of her privacy; besides, more than likely there wasn't anything really wrong with her that a little more time couldn't fix. But still, the university apparently thought that signs of depression were serious. Maybe Tania should have professional advice.

Depression Triggers

A number of situations could make a student feel depressed—blowing an exam, breaking off a relationship, or losing a friend or family member. These episodes are normal, and the intense feelings of sadness and grief pass relatively uneventfully and usually do not interfere with everyday life. Depression is different.

Depression is both a physical disease affecting the brain and an emotional and environmental disorder. Researchers believe that depression causes the parts of the brain that regulate mood, thinking, sleep, appetite, and behavior to function abnormally.[22] In addition, neurotransmitters (chemicals used by brain cells to communicate) appear to be out of balance.[23]

The precise cause of the brain abnormalities is uncertain; however, there is evidence suggesting that in some cases it could be genetic.[24]

Depression is often triggered by stressful life events. This may explain why one in seven college students on campus may be battling depression.[25] People suffering from depression may experience a host of psychological and physical symptoms, such as sadness, anxiety, fatigue, difficulty concentrating or remembering, and chronic aches and pains not explained by another physical condition.[26] The symptoms of depression often interfere with daily life and normal functioning.[27] They can be especially debilitating for students. The good news is that many of the common problems associated with depression are treatable.[28] The bad news is that many students do not seek help because they do not realize that the problems they are experiencing are the result of a disease, or if they do, they may feel embarrassed to talk to a professional. What's worse is that untreated depression may put a person at higher risk for suicidal ideations.

Suicide is the third leading cause of death for young people between the ages of fifteen and twenty-four.[29] An estimated 1,100 college students commit suicide each year, although the number of suicide attempts is much higher.[30] The National Institute for Mental Health estimates that for every suicide death, there are an estimated twelve to twenty-five nonfatal suicide attempts. The link between suicide and depression is strong. In fact, two-thirds of those who die by suicide suffer from depression.[31]

Sonam's suite mate Tania was definitely exhibiting classic signs of depression. The two friends used to do many things together—go to restaurants, attend campus events, and party. However, since Tania's unexpected breakup with her boyfriend, she no longer desired to hang out with Sonam. She did not desire to do much of anything. Put in an awkward situation, Sonam was concerned for her friend's well-being, but at the same time she did not want to overreact or invade Tania's privacy. Complicating the situation was the fact that Tania was exhibiting abnormal behavior around the same time another student had attempted to commit suicide—or at least there was enough circumstantial evidence to assume it was an unsuccessful suicide attempt.

When students have an episode of depression, they are often unaware that their behavior has changed.[32] Concerned roommates, friends, and residence hall advisers may be the first to confront depressed students about changes in their behavior and mental well-being. Since depressed students may not recognize their condition, friends who recognize the symptoms can be instrumental in encouraging intervention. While there is a chance that conversations might not yield any meaningful result or might offend, students will usually turn to a friend if they are struggling emotionally.

HOOK-UP CULTURE

Over the last decade, there has been a significant shift in the attitudes of college students toward sexual relationships. Many students no longer use traditional dating as the primary means of beginning romantic or sexual relationships. Instead, they are hooking up.[33] Hooking up is a casual sexual encounter that occurs between people ranging from complete strangers to brief acquaintances to longtime friends. In terms of sexual behavior, a hook up can be "just kissing, sexual touching, oral sex, or sexual intercourse."[34] The hallmark of hooking up is that the encounter has no strings attached.[35] The hook-up partners usually do not seek a committed relationship, although the same partners may repeatedly hook up over a period of time.

Jacob

Six months into school, Jacob hadn't decided whether he was living a dream or going through hell. From all objective signs, college life had treated him well. He was in great shape, had made a ton of friends without having to join a fraternity and pay the expensive dues, and had managed to keep his grades well over a 3.0—an arrangement that especially pleased his parents. But most impressive to his friends, he had managed to keep a steady stream of dates and other female companionship almost from the start. It had come as somewhat of a surprise to him at first. He was decently athletic and people had told him he was fun to be with, but he never was one of the really cool kids in high school. But it had all come together in college, and he now was the one who always found some new cute girl at parties.

It had started innocently enough. At a party he had attended at the beginning of the year, he had hit it off with Monica, a beautiful slim girl who, by the end of the night, was sitting in his lap and laughing at his jokes. As the party wound down, she had turned and looked at him through glassy eyes and told him she wasn't finished having fun yet. One thing led to another, and the night ended with her staying over in Jacob's room. They didn't have sex, but certainly had enough fun to have embarrassed her mother. They had gotten up the next morning feeling a little embarrassed and really awkward, and Monica slipped out without talking to him.

At first, the experience fried Jacob's nerves enough to make him gun-shy around girls for the next couple of weeks. But that quickly faded as he realized that he had a special knack for being able to make girls like him—and act on those feelings. He soon found himself making a game out of it, challenging himself to find at least one girl at every party who would make out with him, even if things didn't go all the way. Even when it did, the relationship rarely lasted past the first night. Realizing the feelings of awkwardness that went along with it, Jacob was eager to sever ties completely with each of the girls he met.

Initially, he worried about that part of the hook ups, that the girls would get all crazy over one-night stands. A few times he tried talking to them early on and explaining that he wasn't looking for anything serious. But as the school year went on, he found that was less and less of a concern. *They oughta know, right?* he reasoned. *None of this is supposed to be anything serious.*

But by the beginning of the second semester, Jacob had started to feel that his routine wasn't the dream he had thought it to be. After ducking out of a girl's dorm room one Sunday morning and hearing her sobbing with the sheets wrapped around her as he shut the door, he realized he couldn't hide the twinge of guilt he had felt for a while. He knew very well that this one in particular thought there was something to his attentions the previous night—and he hadn't done anything to discourage that perception.

Worse still was the scare he had about a month ago when he got an angry text from a random hook up with that awful *p* word—*pregnant*. He about flipped before realizing a few hours later that she was just mad and knew how to make that anger really felt. But the sensation still shook him up a bit.

By the end of year one, Jacob was in an impossible situation. He was the envy of all of his guy friends, liked by all of his female friends, but he was absolutely miserable. No one would be sympathetic to his problems of finding willing hook ups on a regular basis. His buddies would be shocked and amused by the possibility. He himself didn't see any way to quit. The sex was out there for the taking, and he had a ready way to do it. But the baggage that went with it was a heavy burden to bear.

The New Sexual Revolution

A discussion of civility in the context of a hook up may seem unusual. After all, if two consenting adults choose to have a one-night stand, that's their prerogative. While it is beyond the scope of this book to determine whether hooking up is good or bad, the practice creates more nuanced conflicts that intersect with the concept of civility. There is some ambiguity associated with hooking up. A hook up can range from intimate kissing to sexual intercourse. With such a broad array of possible outcomes, confusion about how far a hook up should go can create problems. If the hook-up partners have differing expectations, sexual assault could be the outcome, especially if alcohol is involved.[36]

A sexual encounter will be considered a rape if the victim does not consent or is unable to consent due to intoxication. Obviously, if someone is passed out drunk, she cannot consent to sex; however, determining how drunk is too drunk to consent is not always clear-cut. A sexual assault may occur when there is a power differential in the hook up and one partner forces the other to engage in sexual activity against the other partner's will. These examples may seem more like instances of bad judgment or an unintentional mistake perhaps caused by intoxication. Nonetheless, sex without consent is rape, not a hook up.

Hooking up also intersects with civility in that it is associated with a number of risk factors that can be devastating to the hook-up partners. For example, hooking up can increase the chances of an unwanted pregnancy. Jacob had this scare when one of his random hook ups texted she was pregnant. It ended up being a prank, but the incident illustrated how a one-night stand can quickly transition to a truly life-changing event. Another risk is contracting a sexually transmitted disease, which can spread to others and may have serious health repercussions. Finally, there may be a psychological toll on students who hook up. For example, a study conducted by the American Sociological Association found that students who hook up get lower grades and have more school-related problems than students who abstain from sex or are in committed relationships.[37] In Jacob's multiple hook ups, he found himself in a number of awkward situations. This awkwardness is not uncommon. Some believe it may drive students to drink more, contributing to the alcohol problem on many campuses.[38]

7

It were not best that we should all think alike; it is difference of opinion that makes horse races.

—Mark Twain

DIVERSITY

The first colleges established in the United States were essentially homogeneous institutions, enrolling men from elite families of European descent. Separate colleges for women followed. African-Americans did not have access to higher education—many were still subjected to legalized slavery. However, this all began to change in 1837 when Oberlin College became the first to enroll both men and women and one of the first to admit African-American students. Since Oberlin cracked the gender and racial barriers, institutions of higher education have often found themselves in the center of issues involving social change.

Over the last two centuries, colleges and universities have had to grapple with how to unlock educational and employment opportunities to underrepresented populations, including individuals of different sexes, races, religions, national origins, disabilities, and sexual orientations. The impetus behind these struggles and eventual changes was a desire to provide equal access to higher education and to create college campuses that were as diverse as the citizens of America. When institutions revised their policies to become more inclusive or respond to societal changes, they often met opposition. When some were slow to respond, they sometimes were required by legal and legislative action to effectuate change.

Today there is broad consensus in higher education that diversity in student bodies, faculty, and staff is vital to the education experience.

According to a study conducted by Patricia Gurin at the University of Michigan, diverse learning environments help students communicate and work effectively with people of varied backgrounds and cultures. These skills are essential for college graduates in an increasingly complex and interconnected world. Learning in a diverse environment prepares students to thrive in the global market place.[1] Diversity also improves classroom discussion, enhancing the experience for all participants. Faculty and students from diverse backgrounds provide unique insights into subject matter based on their cultures, beliefs, and experiences. Exposure to a diverse student body also promotes cross-cultural understanding, an important goal for furthering civility.

The integration of diverse populations on campus can also create unique civility challenges. On campus, students may confront stereotypes or prejudices they have not previously examined. They will need to learn how to live in a community of people from varied backgrounds, beliefs, and values. Although differences can polarize and create rifts, a more productive and civil approach is to strive to understand and respect the differences.

CONFRONTING STEREOTYPES AND PREJUDICE

It is very difficult to avoid stereotypes. They exist to some degree at almost every level of society. A stereotype is a generalized assumption that all members of a certain group possess the same qualities and characteristics. For example, common stereotypes hold that all blondes are flighty and all Asians are good at math. Stereotypes overlook the individuality of a person and presume that everyone of a certain demographic group has the same characteristics, values, opinions, or behaviors. The end result is typically an over generalization, which can lead to unmerited bias and even prejudice and discrimination. Clearly, not all blondes are stupid and not all Asians are mathematicians, yet people often perceive others based on overly broad stereotypes.

Overcoming stereotypes and prejudices is essential to achieving an inclusive and diverse community, but the harmonious integration of diverse groups can prove to be extremely challenging. Differences between groups can create schisms that may further perpetuate stereotypes and lead to prejudice and discrimination. While most people do not consider themselves to be prejudiced, people may continue to associate negative stereotypes with certain groups. Lurking below the surface, the stereotypes are often exposed unintentionally. If offensive stereotypes are exhibited on campus, members of the stereotyped group are likely to respond in opposition regardless of the intention, especially if those stereotypes are racial or ethnic. Antonio and Sonam discovered that ethnic stereotypes and satire do not always mix.

Antonio

It never occurred to Antonio just where this thing would end up.

It had started innocently enough during a meeting. Rob, one of the sophomore fraternity brothers, had suggested a new party theme. Well, maybe *innocently* isn't the right term—after all, Rob's actual suggestion was a "dirty Mexican party." He didn't have an actual hook, but he thought it would be hilarious to get everyone to dress up in sombreros and blankets with small fake mustaches and serve tequila shots with Tecate and Corona beer. Really, in the grand scheme of fraternity parties, it was a pretty tame one.

The guys planning the event thought it sounded great, but at least a couple were smart enough to sense that it could create some trouble. The last thing they wanted was to create any friction with the university administration over something as stupid as a party theme. But the idea itself seemed salvageable. Two of the older brothers, Brandon and Reese, came up with a two-part plan. First, they would choose a name less likely to drum up any serious controversy. Second, they would run it all past their resident ethnic representative.

Step one was easy enough. A few minutes on Google led to the discovery of Pancho Villa, a turn of the century Mexican outlaw and folk hero who seemed to be conveniently sporting a long, thin black mustache and sombrero in most of his surviving pictures. This character seemed like a great fit.

Step two was a little more complicated.

When Brandon and Reese walked over to Antonio one evening after a chapter meeting, he instantly knew something was up. The older guys were nice, but definitely weren't close friends. Antonio had to wait to find out what they wanted, as neither seemed interested in getting to it.

After a few awkward minutes discussing parties and football, Brandon cleared his throat. "Hey, listen, we got something we have to ask you about."

"Sure," Antonio replied just a little hesitantly.

The guys looked at each for a second. "Okay, we've got a plan for a party coming up," Reese finally spit out, "but we got to have some input on whether it's going to seriously tick off anyone."

Antonio definitely was paying attention by now.

"It's a Pancho Villa party. Sombreros, tequila, iconic mustaches, the works. All in good fun—you know, just another reason to drink."

"Ha, yeah, sounds great," Antonio replied. In reality, he had started to piece together exactly where this was headed, but he wanted to draw it out a bit longer.

The guys looked at each other again. "Well, yeah, it will be a hell of a lot of fun," Brandon started, "but do you think we'll catch some flack from anyone about it?"

Antonio could hardly keep from laughing. But he kept it going a bit longer.

"Aw, how do I know? Why are y'all asking me?"

Now the older guys were visibly uncomfortable. "Look, man, we just gotta know. Are we going to offend any of the Mexicans or student groups or anything?" Reese finally asked.

Antonio looked at them really hard for an uncomfortable moment, then finally burst out in long-restrained laughter. "Ha! You guys are so crazy. Look, first of all, I'm Puerto Rican—not Mexican. But more than that, you really think that anyone cares about this party theme any more than the others? We got by with White Trash night and our Party in the Hood, right?"

Brandon and Reese laughed a little, reddening slightly. "Hey, chill out. I know this is all messed up. We just had to run it by someone who might have some idea how this will play out on campus."

"Well, I can't promise anything. But I also can't imagine it being a problem."

Famous last words.

In reality, Pancho Villa night never even got off the ground. One Facebook invitation was the extent of the idea. Rob was given free rein to put his idea into pictures and words, and he took advantage of it, inviting guests to "sport their best spic-and-span mustaches in the most excellent bandito way." Pancho Villa's picture was redrawn to include a bottle of tequila falling out of his back pocket and a border security guard chasing him. The wall quickly devolved into a string of inappropriate jokes.

All of this might have remained somewhat boorish behavior had it not hit the campus at large. One pledge made the mistake of inviting a girl he had been seeing for just a few days to the party. Shortly after she received the invitation, pictures of him making out with some other girl hit Facebook. Enraged, she decided to hit exactly where it hurt—by accepting the party invitation and then extending it to everyone in the Student Organizations office of the Student Government Association and all members of the International Students Club, called the ISC.

The result was a firestorm. The ISC immediately called for a public apology and campus discipline against the fraternity and wrote a very stinging condemnation in a letter to the campus newspaper, which decided to wade into the fray with its own rebuke of the party theme. The fraternity had the sense to cancel the party immediately and go on public radio silence. But on a new, private page dedicated to the doomed party theme, the previously objectionable content quickly ratcheted up to downright nasty. Instead of just jokes, pages and pages of comments were in full-out xenophobia territory, spitting out all kinds of venomous condemnations of the reasons for the party's demise.

Antonio was almost in a state of shock. Something way down in his gut had told him that maybe the theme wasn't the best idea when Brandon and Reese had pitched it to him at first, but his rationalization to them—his looking at the other edgy party themes that had come and gone without controversy—was genuine. No way this party was anything worse than the others.

I mean, it was funny, right? Despite his Latino heritage and his distinctively darker skin, Antonio was always inclined to look for the humor in these situations. These same fraternity brothers who were now being accused of being the most vile and racist beings on campus were the same ones who made fun of *everyone*—their parents, their neighbors, their girlfriends, their dates, everyone who dressed like them, everyone who didn't dress like them, everyone who went to church, everyone who didn't go to church, everyone on the whole campus. *None of it was anywhere near as bad as what they say to each other.*

Antonio couldn't help feeling that it was especially ridiculous for him to be caught up in this. The university had a tiny Latino student population to begin with and only a very small portion of that was Mexican. If anything, he belonged to a tiny class of students who could claim some sort of valid outrage over something offensive.

Now here he was, stuck on a seven-person panel with two other fraternity brothers, three members of the International Students Club, and a moderator, getting ready to "discuss the tensions and the issue" in a roundtable discussion as part of the university's discipline.

Sonam

Sonam sat right across the table. She was equally shocked to be there, but only because she assumed that anyone of sound mind would have known better than to create a party like the doomed one now being discussed.

As a member of the ISC, she had gotten the invitation as soon as it was broadcast to the group at large. Not one of them knew the girl who had sent it, but assumed that someone else in the group did; they had no clue that it was part of a bigger scheme for personal revenge. Not that it really mattered, of course. While the fraternity might not have planned such a widespread broadcast of its plans, the party and the theme weren't a secret by any means.

As Sonam watched the three brothers walk into the room, she recognized one of them as being in one of her classes. The class had over 250 students, so it wasn't a personal relationship by any means, but he had appeared decently intelligent and responsive the few times he had been on call. *Why on earth would he go through with this kind of stunt?* she wondered.

For Sonam, the entire saga had a personal ring to it. Throughout middle school, she had regularly come home sobbing to her parents after a rough day of teasing about her dark skin and then stilted English. Seventh graders were amazingly vicious in their insults, and buoyed by their own self-doubts, they had no reservations about pulling out anything they had in teasing her. Never mind that the insults were often clumsy and even absurd when applied to her situation—they stung nonetheless.

As the years went by, Sonam grew a bit more thick-skinned. She also made friends, developed a natural West Coast dialect and accent, and learned to ignore the worst of the teasing. By high school, it wasn't too much of a problem.

But college had effectively put her back a few years. Gone were the nice comforts of a familiar crowd, and once again she felt treated as conspicuously "different" from many of her classmates, despite having almost everything but her skin color in common with them.

Those feelings led her to join the ISC in the first place. Although Sonam had lived in the country and in the culture for more than seven years, she still vividly remembered the pain of trying to adjust to such radically new surroundings. She figured that one of the best things she could do was to help others less acquainted with American culture make the most out of college. At first, she was a little tentative—after all, she really had more in common with members of other student organizations than the international students in ISC who had just arrived in the United States for the first time.

It had turned out to be a great decision. Sonam quickly made friends with other members in the ISC, and it had become her primary social network at school. Little of her time in the organization was devoted to formal "international student" activities—more than anything else, they were just students and friends who had enough in common to enjoy each other's company.

But this Pancho Villa fiasco was different. This was the sort of thing that called for ISC response. Pretty much what the Alphas had done was fire an open salvo of hostility toward students of Mexican and Latino descent on campus. Everything about the Pancho Villa party screamed a message of ridicule and unwelcome, from the ethnic stereotypes to the racial jokes. As a foreign-born student, Sonam didn't just feel that the party was offensive in general—she felt personally insulted by the vulgar "they're so different and stupid" implications in such an event.

As the Alpha brothers filed in, Sonam immediately noticed the distinctively darker skin and dark features of one of the brothers. She couldn't tell for sure, but he definitely looked like he was Latino. A strange mixture of anger and puzzlement seeped in her brain. *Why is he here? Doesn't he get what this is all about? Couldn't he have said something?*

Ethnic Stereotypes

What causes people to develop stereotypes? The precise reasons are very complex and involve a number of psychological and environmental factors. Some social psychologists believe that stereotypes are an involuntary response to our natural tendency to categorize.[2] People tend to group others based on easily identifiable categories, such as age, race, gender, religion, or political affiliation.[3] Over time people learn to associate certain characteristics with certain groups.[4] Stereotypes may also be developed when the members of one group have little contact with other outside groups.[5] The lack of integration between diverse groups may make it easier for stereotypes to be formed. Many believe that the media reinforce stereotypes.[6] Movies, television, and advertising frequently incorporate stereotypes.

The ethnic stereotypes associated with the Pancho Villa party that Antonio's fraternity intended to host were supposed to be a joke, but the party blurred the line between humorous and offensive. The fraternity probably did not intend to offend Latino students or anyone else on campus. To them, it was just another opportunity to party but with a Mexican flare. After all, the fraternity had gotten away with similar edgy themes.

When Sonam received the invitation, she did not see the humor. In fact, she was deeply offended. Although Sonam was not Mexican, she had been the victim of negative stereotypes while she was growing up. Sonam's turbulent integration into American culture attracted her to the International Students Club. She wanted to help other foreign-born students adjust to life in the States. When Sonam discovered that Antonio, a Latino-looking student, was in on the party, she was shocked and wondered why he did not intervene.

It is interesting and telling that Antonio and Sonam, who were both minority students, processed the Pancho Villa party differently. Antonio saw the party as no big deal. To him, it was an insignificant party theme, one of many conceived by his fraternity. Sonam saw the party theme as sending a message of ridicule and unwelcome not only to Latino students, but also to all foreign-born students.

Like Antonio, many would dismiss ethnic stereotyping, such as the Pancho Villa party, as harmless or even entertaining. While the direct impact of the firestorm created by the party would be difficult to measure, it did trigger and perhaps perpetuate negative stereotypes about Mexicans and about those groups on campus that opposed the party.

At its core, the Pancho Villa party was just a joke. However, issues involving ethnicity and race are complex. The fact that the fraternity had first run the party theme past Antonio demonstrates that it recognized the potential for the party to offend. In a community as ethnically and racially diverse as a college campus, more consideration should have been given to the potential impact of the party. Was it respectful to others in the campus community? Did it have the potential to offend? Did it have the potential of perpetuating negative stereotypes and discrimination? The answers to these questions would be difficult to answer on the front end. Anticipating how the campus community would respond to a satirical event is not always easy. The aftermath of the Pancho Villa party proved to be a disaster for the community. Students were offended, negative stereotypes were perpetuated, and the community was divided. Ethnic and racial stereotyping is not a laughing matter.

COEXISTING PEACEFULLY

Achieving meaningful diversity may be most challenging between groups that are diametrically opposed. For example, it might be rare for student Democratic and Republican clubs to work together constructively or for Jewish and Muslim student groups to collaborate and address problems on campus. Campuses are full of diverse and often conflicting groups, posing a number of unique challenges for campus communities. How can groups with drastically different beliefs, opinions, and values coexist? Should they simply attempt to stay out of each other's way to avoid conflict? Is there a way for divergent groups to demonstrate, or oppose a demonstration, that is respectful to the entire community, yet does not dilute their message or beliefs?

Balancing the needs of conflicting groups can be very messy. Emotions run high when people passionately support or oppose an issue. Many times sound judgment and reason take a backseat to provocative and offensive outbursts. Jacob experienced this when he participated in a protest against discrimination toward gay, lesbian, bisexual, and transgender (GLBT) students.

Jacob

As the spring semester was drawing to a close, Jacob had one important date looming on his calendar: April 12. But it wasn't for a paper or a final—instead, it was this year's Day of Silence, a campus wide student protest against discrimination toward gay, lesbian, bisexual, and transgender interests. Jacob had several friends in the organization and had good-naturedly agreed to participate. As the days counted down, though, he started to dread the event.

As a whole, Jacob was pretty ambivalent politically. He didn't consider himself attached to any political party or in alignment with any major groups—frankly, he just tried to stay away as much as possible. Politics ruined otherwise perfectly good relationships. But this was a little different. Abby, one of his closest female friends, had pleaded with him at length to join the protest with her for a single hour time slot on the quad, and now that he had agreed, he really didn't want to go back on his word.

But Jacob had become reluctant to participate because he learned how the event had gone in the past. Apparently, last year a student group calling itself Students Against Gay Marriage (SAGM) had thought it fitting to schedule its own protest on the same day as the Day of Silence protestors, going so far as to book a spot on the quad exactly opposite the GLBT group to man a table. While it had started mildly enough—essentially a flurry of brochure passing by both groups, leading hundreds of uninterested and hurried students to avoid the walkway entirely—things went downhill from there. Eventually, the two groups managed to start having "discussions." Those apparently didn't go so well and led to shouting matches. When a few university police officers arrived with the intent to keep the peace and enforce the assigned protest areas, the SAGM members decided on a new tactic. They steadfastly—and impertinently—toed the boundary line for their booth and began hurling inflammatory slurs and opinions, somewhat blurring the distinction between the two. When a campus administrator came out to ask them to show some decency and respect, they started shouting at her as a group, decrying her "censorship" and proclaiming their rights to free speech. Needless to say, the entire incident left a bad taste in everyone's mouth.

Jacob had no interest in being a part of that kind of spectacle. He was naturally nonconfrontational, and it wouldn't even surprise him if he knew somebody who might show up to support an opposing position—he did have a pretty big network of friends. But upon being assured that steps had been taken to keep the peace this year, he decided to keep his promise to Abby and work the table for an hour in the afternoon.

As soon as his materials class let out at 12:50, he hurried over to the quad. The lunch hour was dying down, and there really wasn't much foot traffic. *This won't be too bad*, he thought.

"Hey, Jake!" Abby had seen him arrive. "I'm so glad you came."

"Yep, said I would." He looked around. "Any drama this year?"

"Nothing like last year," Abby said with a laugh. "The school had the sense to put the whackos down farther this time." She nodded at booths way down on the other side of the concourse. "Probably the right move."

"I bet it was."

Jacob looked around at the table. Other than the half dozen GLBT protestors, the only other students in sight were two guys sitting on a bench about fifteen feet away with their heads down. They appeared to be in prayer. He turned to Abby. "What's up with those guys?"

Abby shrugged. "They've been here all morning. Couple of religious fundies or something, trying to save our souls from hell. Haven't said a word, though."

That's a bit obnoxious, thought Jacob. *Anywhere on campus they could do that. Why right here?*

A rush of students came by shortly to make it to 1:15 classes. As 1:20 rolled around, the quad emptied out again. Some of the GLBT protestors started getting restless. One sauntered over to the two guys on the bench.

"Hey, what do you think you're doing over here? Being holy?"

One of the guys looked up, obviously uncomfortable. "Um, no, not at all, really..." he started.

"Then why don't you leave?" It was sort of a suggestion.

The two looked at each other. "I don't think so," the first replied quietly.

By that time, another protestor had come over to the scene. "Look, on a day like today, the last thing we need is a couple of bigots over here making everyone uncomfortable. Or is that normal for you? You a bunch of fascists or something?"

A crowd was gathering. The other protestors had drifted toward the noise. While most of them didn't seem comfortable with what was happening, none of them made any move to stop it, either.

Jacob was eternally grateful to be occupied in handing out flyers at the moment. He really had no idea what to think about what was going on. It was both odd and a little rude that two guys had decided that this was the appropriate time and place for a public prayer demonstration. But they hadn't really bothered anyone—the taunting seemed like overkill.

GLBT And Diversity

When diversity is discussed, racial and ethnic diversity are typically the first examples that come to mind. However, diversity encompasses more than just race and ethnicity. It is multidimensional and includes factors such as sex, religion, sexual orientation, and gender identity.[7] Today some of the biggest hot button diversity issues involve the inclusion and acceptance of gay, lesbian, bisexual, and transgender people into the mainstream.

Like other minority groups on campus, GLBT groups have been subjected to negative stereotypes, prejudice, and discrimination over the years. Many people have moral reservations about homosexuality and transgenderism and may oppose efforts to validate their lifestyles, although negative attitudes toward GLBT people are beginning to change, especially among students. The causes of this shift in opinion are the result of a convergence of a variety of factors, including advocacy and education, particularly at the college level. For example, a recent Gallup Poll found that 75 percent of people between eighteen and thirty-four years old considered homosexuality an acceptable alternative lifestyle.[8] Likewise, transgender people are beginning to gain broader acceptance on college campuses. For example, there is a growing movement among colleges to offer gender-neutral restrooms and housing options, and to expand health insurance plans to accommodate transgender students and employees.[9]

At a micro level, Jacob found himself in the middle of the cultural debate over same-sex marriage. Although he did not have strong feelings about gay marriage, he found himself picking sides when he volunteered to pass out literature at the Day of Silence protest. When Jacob volunteered, he was unaware that at last year's event, a competing group decided to demonstrate simultaneously. The demonstrations got so out of hand that it took police intervention to keep the peace. Jacob dreaded the thought that the protest might turn into an unproductive fiasco.

Fortunately for Jacob, the Day of Silence protest was relatively uneventful. However, emotions flared when protesters confronted two students who appeared to be praying near the event. Although the praying students did not interfere with the event, their presence seemed to vex some protestors, resulting in a hostile confrontation.

Accommodating diversity requires more than mere coexisting with differing groups and populations. It requires an attempt to understand why someone has a different perspective or opinion. As with civility, it requires an effort to speak less and listen more. While the Day of Silence protesters and the praying students held divergent views, as members of the campus community, they might have learned more if they started the discussion with an attitude of mutual understanding and respect.

ACHIEVING A DIVERSE EDUCATIONAL ENVIRONMENT

Achieving diversity in any environment does not occur automatically. People tend to group themselves based on similarities, everything from race and religion to socioeconomic status. Efforts to integrate people from diverse backgrounds are often awkward for everyone involved. Some may harbor concerns that the integration of people dissimilar from themselves— in student organizations or academic programs—will create conflict or dilute the group's effectiveness based on the lack of commonality.

Although attempts to achieve diversity may seem forced or cause discomfort, research suggests that learning in a diverse environment has significant benefits. Diverse learning environments help students to think in deeper and in more complex ways,[10] and they prepare students to become active participants in a pluralistic and democratic society.[11] Achieving diversity creates significant challenges.

Lindsey

When it came to obligations, Lindsey had always been somewhat of a glutton for punishment. In high school she had been the classic overachiever, committing to everything from yearbook staff to the cross-country team to cheerleading while maintaining an A average the whole time. It hadn't taken long to carry the same reckless enthusiasm into college, where she promptly joined a sorority and the freshman office of the Student Government Association. Realizing that she had really enjoyed yearbook in high school—and thinking that she might be interested in doing some sort of photography, design, or writing work as a career— Lindsey also joined the campus newspaper as a staff writer.

All told, it was a good decision. She really enjoyed the work and managed to find the time to be a contributing member without having it totally consume her life. Near the end of the spring semester, she successfully ran for production editor, a position that gave her a leadership office with the paper.

The first order of business for the year was a second round of recruitment for entry-level positions. It was always a bit of work finding enough willing and capable people to staff the paper in any given year, and the past semester the staff had been particularly thin. The eight officers scheduled a meeting to discuss their approach for attracting new talent.

The meeting took a different turn than expected, though. James, a quiet, older student who made a good editor in chief, started things off by pulling out a letter he had recently gotten in the newspaper's campus mailbox. He read it to the group:

> Dear Mr. Golding:
>
> I am writing on behalf of a campus organization that—for the time being and for understandable reasons—wishes to remain anonymous. Its concerns must be voiced; however, I am well aware of a pattern of intentional and invidious racial discrimination the *Campus Guardian* has engaged in for a period of almost a decade. As I'm sure you're well aware, your organization has not selected a single African-American student to fill either an entry-level or editor position for the past three years. As a result, your newspaper—to the best of my knowledge—is now comprised of 95 percent nonminority students, a number far disproportionate to their representation on this campus.
>
> This letter is meant to be a warning that such continued conduct cannot and will not be tolerated. We do not want to institute adversarial action, but will not hesitate if it proves necessary. Please advise us immediately of any plans the newspaper has to remedy the situation.
>
> /s/ Prof. Ronald Kerling

Everyone around the table just sat there quietly. A few of the officers furtively glanced around as if noticing for the first time that pretty much everyone at the table looked similar, at least in skin and eye color.

Eventually, the quiet dissolved into a somewhat noisy buzz. The general reaction was that the professor was being entirely unfair and unreasonable. True, the staff didn't exactly reflect the composition of the student body, but they *definitely* never had purposefully excluded any qualified applicants. Besides, half of them hadn't even made a selection decision, so this really seemed unfair to blame on them.

After a while, most of the steam had blown off, and the students were starting to be realistic about the problem at hand. At the very least, they had a situation that looked really bad, and they needed to take steps to address it. James asked everyone to go around the table and come up with a suggestion for what the newspaper could do to address the problems noted in Professor Kerling's letter so they could offer him a credible response.

Lindsey was very relieved to go second—when plausible solutions were still plentiful. "Maybe the easiest thing would be to just increase our minority applicant pools with some recruiting," she offered. "You know, make some formal pitches to some of the African-American student groups that we're looking for qualified applicants and we offer this and that, or whatever." Everyone else at the table nodded. That much seemed relatively easy and painless.

But as the conversation made its way around the table, the solutions started becoming less and less clear-cut. One editor suggested that the newspaper reserve one spot for a minority applicant out of this application cycle—and as many more in the future as necessary—and be done with it. No one seemed very enthusiastic about the idea, though, so it was tabled for the time being.

Others didn't go quite so far, but definitely trended in that direction. One suggestion was that they simply conduct face-to-face interviews with every candidate and have a grading rubric that included a score for diversity. Another was that instead of leaving the meaning of diversity up to the staff members (and, almost by default, defining it in terms of skin color), the applications ought to have a section for diversity where the applicants could describe why they are diverse. This seemed a bit less quota like, at least.

Lindsey was at a loss about what they ought to do. On the one hand, it was clear that there was a problem and it needed some sort of fix. On the other, diversity was quite a heavy topic to be dealt with through such crude approaches.

Racial Diversity

The United States is one of the most diverse societies, yet most Americans from different racial and ethnic groups tend to lead separate lives. With the majority of neighborhoods and schools segregated based on race, people from diverse backgrounds rarely have sustained or meaningful contacts.[12] As a result, people seldom benefit from the exposure to the ideas and perspectives of people from differing backgrounds. This lack of contact may also foster misconceptions and mistrust between differing racial groups and can contribute to the perpetuation of stereotypes.

While there are many different efforts to achieve greater racial diversity, none have been as hotly contested as affirmative action programs. Colleges and universities have used them to achieve diversity. Over the years affirmative action has taken on many forms. For example, some affirmative action programs have utilized separate tracks or admission requirements for minority students. For schools that use a point system to determine admission, some programs awarded minority students a certain number of points based only on their minority status. Other affirmative action programs reserved a certain number of seats exclusively for minority students. Some have praised these initiatives as leveling the playing field, and others have vehemently objected to them by claiming that such practices are reverse discrimination.[13]

Since the late 1970's, challenges to affirmative action have resulted in several high-profile U.S. Supreme Court decisions. According to the Supreme Court, race may be considered as long as there is a compelling government interest and the program is narrowly tailored to foster educational diversity.[14] While the Court has found that a diverse student body is a compelling government interest, it has rejected programs that isolate minorities from competition, use separate tracks for minority and nonminority admission, or rely on quotas. The Court has also struck down affirmative action programs that utilize rigid variables, such as scores or point systems.[15] According to the Court, a narrowly tailored race-conscious program involves individualized considerations of race in a flexible, nonmechanical way and must consider "all the ways an applicant might contribute to a diverse educational environment."[16]

Lindsey experienced some of the difficulties of achieving racial diversity when a faculty member challenged the student makeup of the campus newspaper. The faculty member saw the lack of minority representation on the newspaper as an act of "intentional and invidious racial discrimination." The students on the newspaper had never really noticed that there were no minority students contributing to the paper. The issue was not on their radar.

Being accused of intentionally discriminating against minorities by a university official is a serious charge. The conundrum was, how could they make a good faith effort to recruit minority students? The threatening tone of the letter created urgency for the group to act—and act fast. Although various ideas were discussed, there seemed to be no clear-cut answer. How could the campus newspaper promote racial integration without appearing condescending toward the minority students it intended to recruit? Lindsey's suggestion to reach out to some of the minority student groups on campus was a helpful beginning.

For members of a campus community, demonstrating mutual respect for differing groups is essential to achieving meaningful diversity. College campuses are becoming increasingly diverse communities. Efforts to embrace diversity, celebrate difference, and engage in respectful discourse—even when the differences are significant—can be very rewarding and, if appropriately carried out, can promote civility.

8

A person is a person through other people.
—Nontombi Naomi Tutu, 2010

FACING CIVILITY

Thousands of American college students *do* look, sound, and think like Antonio, Lindsey, Sonam, and Jacob and face many of the same civility dilemmas. To prepare for some of these inevitable situations, students should anticipate potential problems and contemplate how they would respond. Those thoughts need to be guided by the ethics and morals they have adopted as their own from years of training and instruction by parents, teachers, religious figures, mentors, and others. This discussion isn't intended to be groundbreaking in that regard. Most of these students would probably acknowledge that being civil is consistent with their notions of ethical conduct; after all, the Golden Rule has long been observed to transcend cultural and religious boundaries.[1] The angle presented in these pages isn't so much a call for students to be more civil as much as an illustration of what civil and uncivil conduct *looks like* when applied in the college setting

In these pages we've covered a wide variety of issues, ranging from obscene taunts at athletic events to modern campus hook-up culture. Admittedly, the variety stretches conventional notions of civility; no existing book on civility probably would be so bold in trying to cover so many issues under one banner. But the broadness of the topic here is intentional. We feel that civility—properly defined as including a combination of considerate conduct toward others embodied in the Golden Rule and a notion of civic duty for the community—is a broad topic. Student behaviors in the classroom, in the dorms, at football games, even in how they treat their own bodies, minds, and spirits all fit into that notion. A narrower conception of civility would contradict the main message of this book: American college students need to make the connection between the morals and values they claim to hold and the practical implications of those values expressed through acts of civility in every part of their lives.

In essence, we propose a new conception of civility for a new generation of college students who are attending a new type of college. Today's college students are simultaneously more engaged with the world around them and less guided by older adults through the experience of their college years. Arguing whether this is a good or a bad development is a dead point by now—it is the reality. So we suggest instead that these students need to combine their aptitude and inclination to interact with the world at large through information, communication, and cultural exchanges with a comprehensive sense of self-responsibility that calls for civil conduct in all parts of their college lives.

There is a lot of good news when it comes to college students and notions of civility. As mentioned earlier in the book, today's college students are more diverse than ever before. That alone reflects a society that is more diverse and more open to people of different races and cultures than the college environment of fifty years ago.

The other good news comes from the interests and involvement of the modern college student. As shown in the University of California, Los Angeles's annual survey of entering college freshmen at hundreds of institutions across the nation, a huge percentage of today's college students consider volunteering and helping others to be an important part of their lives.[2] An equally large portion of students are involved in campus groups— political groups, service organizations, and common interest societies. This sort of involvement fits with the *civitas* notion of civility: college students are serving as involved and contributing members of their communities in order to serve the greater good.

In many respects, this trend should not be surprising. Today's entering college students belong to the Millennial generation, one that is more involved and interconnected than any that preceded it. As discussed in chapter 1, Millennials have found new ways to be connected to their peers and their communities, often with the aid of technologies such as text messaging and social networking websites. But as this level of interconnectedness has opened the door for more encounters with others, the possibility for conflicts of cultures and values has increased as well. As a result, today's students are often thrust in situations where they can perpetuate incivility and disregard for the thoughts, abilities, appearances, and cultures of others through multiple arenas, both in person and online.

In this, we're back where we started—the civility crisis on the modern college campus. Simply saying that students should try to be more civil in everything they do is not going to do much to fix a culture of rude and inconsiderate behavior that has seemed to take deep root over the past few decades. But what might be more successful is to show students how and when opportunities for civil conduct can arise and how they can make the most of them. Again, although this might include some instructions in civility, its real appeal is that such demonstrations of civil conduct are merely manifestations of the moral principles that all of these students recognize and at least nominally embrace. Civil conduct simply requires treating others the way you wish to be treated—with a due regard for individual differences—as well as a sense of duty and responsibility to the community. With appropriate preparation, prompting, and encouragement, college students *can* learn how to actualize these notions of civility and make them part of their lives.

And what about the characters we've used to achieve these ends? There are two temptations for them. First, the most tempting end would be to write them all a neat Epilogue where each makes all or nearly all the right civil choices and goes on to lead an exciting, fulfilling, and enviable life as a result. As appealing as that sounds, we want to avoid it here. We've tried to the best of our ability to make the characters we've presented *real*—in their struggles, their thoughts, their backgrounds, and their emotions. And because they're real, they won't be able to make the perfect choices every time. Even when they do, it might not lead to lives of complete prosperity and happiness. So for now we will avoid giving Antonio, Lindsey, Sonam, and Jacob the storybook endings that we all want deep down for our protagonists.

But the second temptation won't work, either. We could have used our characters as cautionary figures who consistently make poor decisions and thus suffer the consequences. We avoided this, too, because we thought it was unrealistic; most college students want to do the right thing most of the time. So while we won't give them the unrealistic expectation of perfection, we will go so far as to venture that they probably made a good decision in most of the circumstances they faced.

Ultimately, the fates of our four freshmen are in the readers' hands. They all faced very complicated civility dilemmas and could easily be forgiven for making the occasional poor choice—in fact, in a few of the scenarios, the best choice might not even be clear. But the important point is that those choices do come up—and they matter. We hope that in the course of following Antonio, Lindsey, Sonam, and Jacob, you've had the chance to think about some parts of your life and how the question of civility might come up. We hope that thinking ahead about what *you* would do in those scenarios leads you to a working concept of civility that reflects your own judgments and values and enhances your world for the others in it.

About the Author

Kent M. Weeks draws on a wide range of experience in addressing the topic of civility on the college and university campus. He served as a college administrator, taught at The College of Wooster, and for twenty-five years taught undergraduate and graduate students in public policy and school and higher education law at George Peabody College, Vanderbilt University, where he was awarded the Peabody College Roundtable Award for excellence in teaching.

Weeks practices law in Nashville, Tennessee, where he focuses on legal and policy issues affecting higher education and observes his clients wrestling with issues arising from increasing incivility on college campuses. His writing is informed by them and by insights from his students.

He has written several books and published more than sixty articles and papers for scholarly journals and educational publications, and he currently edits *Lex Collegii*, a legal newsletter for colleges and universities. His writings focus on academic and student issues such as student civility, ethical behavior of faculty, plagiarism, privacy, alcohol, drug use, hook-up culture, suicide, and parental rights. He recently completed the book *A Leaner America: Private Choices and Public Policies*, which examines the causes of the startling epidemic of obesity and zeros in on the efforts needed to address this problem.

Weeks consults with colleges throughout the United States and served as general counsel to Africa University in Zimbabwe for more than twenty years. His professional association recently named him as a Fellow in recognition of exceptional scholarship and service on behalf of colleges and universities.

Involved in many community activities, Weeks chaired the first elected School Board for Nashville-Davidson County and was later honored for his work in obtaining a settlement of the twenty-eight-year desegregation litigation.

A Fulbright scholar, Weeks earned a Ph.D. in political science from Case Western Reserve University, a law degree from Duke University, an M.A. from the University of New Zealand, and a B.A. from The College of Wooster in Ohio.

APPENDICES

1.0 College Civility Initiatives

    1.1   Campus Civility Statement, Coe College

    1.2   Respect and Civility in the Campus Community, University of California, Berkeley

    1.3   Civitas: A Community of Civil and Responsible Citizens, American University

    1.4   Diversity, Civility & Equity, University of Chicago

    1.5   Civility Statement, Ocean County College

    1.6   Statement of Civility, Jefferson Community College

2.0 Civility Resources

    2.1   The Civility Pledge, CivilityProject.org

    2.2   The Civility Quiz, PaperClip Communications

    2.3   Elements of Effective Problem Solving, *In Control*, Williams and Williams

3.0 Local Government Civility Initiatives

    3.1   Civility in the Public Square—10 Rules that Work, Institute for Civility in Government

    3.2   Choose Civility Initiative, Howard County, Maryland

    3.3   Resolution Accepting the Nine Tools of Civility, City of Superior, Wisconsin

Appendix 1.0
COLLEGE CIVILITY INITIATIVES

1.1 CAMPUS CIVILITY STATEMENT
Coe College, Cedar Rapids, Iowa

This statement was written by students to address standards of civility and respect within the Coe College community. This statement is a living document and is intended to evolve over time.

We, the members of the Coe College community, expect our campus climate to be safe, mutually supportive, academically encouraging, egalitarian, and tolerant of all its members:

- We expect the academic experience to extend beyond the classroom into our living environment.

- We expect a campus free of incidents that create a hostile living environment.

- We expect a healthy and responsible attitude to accompany all social gatherings.

- We expect that intoxication will not be an excuse for incidents that occur while under the influence.

- We expect that diversity of opinion should be cultivated and encouraged as well as respected within our community.

- We expect that everyone will have the right to be respected for his or her individuality.

- We expect all campus community members to respect the rights of other persons regardless of their actual or perceived: age, color, creed, disability, gender identity, national origin, race religion, sex, or sexual orientation.

A community is made up of individuals who model these standards and hold each other accountable. In order for the community to encompass the goals outlined above, each individual must be responsible and accountable for her or his own actions and words.

www.coe.edu/studentlife/orientation/handbook/civility.htm

1.2 RESPECT AND CIVILITY
IN THE CAMPUS COMMUNITY
University of California, Berkeley, California

The University of California at Berkeley is a public institution of higher education committed to excellence in teaching, research, and public service. Our student body represents the diversity of our state, and will provide its future leaders. Together, the students, faculty, and staff form our campus community, which reflects a variety of backgrounds and cultures. The quality of life on and about the campus is best served by courteous and dignified interaction between all individuals, regardless of sex, ethnic or religious background, sexual orientation, or disability.

Therefore, the administration of this university publicly declares its expectation that all members of the campus community will work to develop and maintain a high degree of respect and civility for the wealth of diversity in which we are all fortunate to live and work together. This civility and respect for diversity ought to flourish in an atmosphere of academic freedom that is considerate and tolerant of the ideas of others. The administration of this University expects you to consult the student code for specific regulations regarding respect and civility.

http://students.berkeley.edu/uga/respect.stm

1.3 CIVITAS: A COMMUNITY OF CIVIL AND RESPONSIBLE CITIZENS

A Campus Life Initiative
American University, Washington, DC

In the Fall of 2003, The Office of Campus Life launched the CIVITAS campaign to encourage civility and responsible citizenship in the AU community. CIVITAS, the Latin word for city, has been chosen as the theme for the campaign because it connotes the kind of environment that shapes us as good citizens and good neighbors.

The mission of the CIVITAS campaign is to heighten our awareness of the relationship between our personal conduct and the quality of campus life. What we do and say always has an effect on others, whether we see it or not. Civility means more than just holding the door open for someone or respecting campus facilities and grounds. It means consistently treating people with consideration and respect. When our behavior is guided by concern for others in our community, we are being civil!

Practicing civility requires thoughtful behavior and continuous refinement of our perceptions of what matters to us and to others. A short checklist of actions can help us move toward more civil conduct:

Choose—We choose how we behave. Make your choices conscious ones by deciding ahead of time how you will act in a situation and rehearsing it in your mind.

Act—Act thoughtfully—as if you were in the other person's shoes!

Reflect—Consider how your actions and words have made others feel. If you have caused harm or discomfort, apologize, and consider how you can modify your behavior the next time.

www.american.edu/ocl/vp/civitas/

1.4 DIVERSITY, CIVILITY & EQUITY

University Statements and Policies

University of Chicago, Chicago, Illinois

Commitment to the University Community

The University of Chicago is a community of scholars dedicated to research, academic excellence, and the pursuit and cultivation of learning. Every member of the University—student, faculty, and staff—makes a commitment to strive for personal and academic integrity; to treat others with dignity and respect; to honor the rights and property of others; to take responsibility for individual and group behavior; and to act as a responsible citizen in a free academic community and in the larger society. Any student conduct, on or off campus, of individuals or groups, that threatens or violates this commitment may become a matter of action within the University's system of student discipline. (Student manual 2009-2010)

. . . .

Civil Behavior in a University Setting

At the University of Chicago, freedom of expression is vital to our shared goal of the pursuit of knowledge, as is the right of all members of the community to explore new ideas and learn from one another. To preserve an environment of spirited and open debate, we should all have the opportunity to contribute to intellectual exchanges and participate fully in the life of the University.

The ideas of different members of the University community will frequently conflict and we do not attempt to shield people from ideas that they may find unwelcome, disagreeable, or even offensive. Nor, as a general rule, does the University intervene to enforce social standards of civility. There are, however, some circumstances in which behavior so violates our community's standards that formal University intervention may be appropriate. Acts of violence, and explicit threats of violence directed at a particular individual that compromise that individual's safety or ability to function within the University setting are direct affronts to the University's values and warrant intervention by University officials. Abusive conduct directed at a particular individual that compromises that individual's ability to function within the University setting and/or that persists after the individual has asked that it stop may also warrant such intervention. Even if formal intervention is not appropriate in a particular situation, abusive or offensive behavior can nonetheless be consistent with the aspirations of the University community, and various forms of informal assistance and counseling are available.

http://civility.uchicago.edu/policies.shtml

1.5 CIVILITY STATEMENT
Ocean County College, Toms River, New Jersey

Ocean County College defines civility primarily as the demonstration of respect for others, basic courtesy, reciprocity (treating others as we wish to be treated), and behaviors that create a positive environment in which to learn and to work.

The Trustees of the College and the College Administration set the tone for civil behavior through their professional conduct and through their leadership of the institution. All members of the college community create a positive environment characterized by considerate and principled conduct.

While no civility statement can guarantee considerate and principled conduct, the values set forth herewith represent institutional ideals and should serve as guide posts:

1. Respect for the work of all persons

2. Courteous discourse (oral, verbal, non-verbal and electronic)

3. Honest interactions and utterances

4. Fair and just treatment

5. Integrity and keeping promises

6. Commitment to the community college philosophy: Access, transfer, career preparation, workforce development, partnering, and community outreach. www.ocean.edu/welcome/mission_vision.htm

7. Open professional communications

8. Diversity, professionalism, and collegiality

9. Free expression of views without meanness or a desire to do harm

10. Tolerance of differing points of view

11. Zero tolerance for any forms of cyber stalking, cyber bullying, or cyber sexual harassment (see the Attorney General's letter)

12. A culture of honor that enhances our students' ethical and moral development and clearly communicates and

consistently adheres to the definitions of and sanctions for
academic dishonesty

These ideas are consistently modeled by those in leadership positions—
in the administration, staff, faculty, and student body—and should provide
direction for all members of the college community.

www.ocean.edu/campus/PAR/civility.htm

1.6 STATEMENT OF CIVILITY
Jefferson Community College, Watertown, New York

Jefferson Community College believes that all persons should be extended civility and respect, regardless of factors such as opinions/view, institutional role, race, religion, ethnicity, disability, gender, sexual orientation or age. Teaching and learning are the focus of Jefferson Community College. Accordingly, the College is committed to creating and maintaining positive learning and working environments both in and out of the academic classroom.

While it is understood that disagreement will and should occur in a collegiate setting, open communication, intellectual integrity, mutual respect for differing viewpoints, freedom from unnecessary disruption/disorder and a climate of civility are important institutional values.

www.sunyjefferson.edu/catalog/campus/civil.html

APPENDIX 2.0
CIVILITY RESOURCES

2.1 THE CIVILITY PLEDGE
CivilityProject.org

In January 2009, [Mark DeMoss] launched CivilityProject.org—a collection of liberals and conservatives, Democrats and Republicans, blacks and whites, and people of various faiths—or no faith—who agree that even in sharp disagreement we should not be disagreeable. . . . Civility should be preferred to incivility and that's why we're inviting everyone who will take the Civility Pledge. It simply says:

- I will be civil in my public discourse and behavior.
- I will be respectful of others whether or not I agree with them.
- I will stand against incivility when I see it.

The core values of the organization include:

- **Civility** in all situations
- **Courage** to do what's right
- **Graciousness** in conduct and speech
- **Honesty** in all communications
- **Integrity** of heart
- **Respect** for the right of others to hold and express views different from my own.

www.civilityproject.org

2.2 THE CIVILITY QUIZ

**A Follow-up to PaperClip Communications'
Audio Conference on Civility Issues, February 4, 2005**

The five main things that spring to mind when I envision a "Civil Campus" are:

1.

2.

3.

4.

5.

Examples of civil behavior that I have witnessed on campus during the past year include:

Examples of uncivil behavior that I have witnessed on campus during the past year include:

Creating a civil campus is important to me because......

What role does respect play here on campus?

I agree/disagree with this statement: The encouragement toward civility will help our students become more engaged, caring citizens of the world. Why?

I agree/disagree with this statement: In the workplace, faculty and staff members here are civil to one another. Why?

Five things I can do in my everyday work/life to be more civil on campus include:

1.

2.

3.

4.

5.

2.3 ELEMENTS OF EFFECTIVE PROBLEM SOLVING

**In Control: No more snapping at your family,
sulking at work, steaming in the grocery line,
seething at meetings, stuffing your frustration.**

Redford Williams and Virginia Williams, Rodale, Inc., 2006

In the book, *In Control*, the authors explore issues related to assisting people learn how to be more in control of their lives. In their discussion of how to resolve problems and implement solutions, they offer strategies— many of which implicitly relate to notions undergirding civility.

Effective problem solving involves seven actions.

Define the problem

Clarify your goals and objectives

List all possible solutions

Make a decision

Implement the decision

Evaluate the outcome

Reconsider options as necessary

www.williamslifeskills.com

APPENDIX 3.0
LOCAL GOVERNMENT CIVILITY INITIATIVES

3.1 INSTITUTE FOR CIVILITY IN GOVERNMENT
Civility in the Public Square—10 Rules that Work, 2007

Donna Bowling, Cassandra Dahnke, and Tomas Spath,

Wingspan Press, Livermore, CA, 2007

The Institute for Civility in Government is a non-profit organization that works to reduce polarization in society. Through educational programs and membership, the Institute aims to build civility in a society that increasingly tilts towards uncivil speech and actions. The Institute provides training based on the rules in the book.

Rule # 1: Know Yourself

Rule # 2: Listen with Your Strength

Rule # 3: Respect: Differences are Enriching

Rule # 4: Listen with Your Mind

Rule # 5: Help Comes from the Most Unexpected Places

Rule # 6: Relationship is Everything

Rule # 7: Listen with Your Heart

Rule # 8: Trust, Trust, Trust

Rule # 9: One is Powerful

Rule # 10: Numbers Count

www.wingspanpress.com

3.2 CHOOSE CIVILITY INITIATIVE
Howard County, Maryland

The Choose Civility Initiative in Howard County was initially inspired by the book, *Choosing Civility: The 25 Rules of Considerate Conduct*, by Dr. P. M. Forni. Howard County has chosen to promote 15 of his rules as guiding ideas and principles that resonate with the community.

Principles of Civility:

Pay attention

Listen

Speak kindly

Assume the best

Respect others' opinions

Respect other people's time and space

Be inclusive

Acknowledge others

Accept and give praise

Apologize earnestly

Assert yourself

Take responsibility

Accept and give constructive criticism

Refrain from idle complaints

Be a considerate guest

www.choosecivility.org

3.3 RESOLUTION ACCEPTING
THE NINE TOOLS OF CIVILITY

Superior City Council, Wisconsin
Resolution R03-12467, September 2, 2003

The resolution grew out of the Speak Your Peace Civility Project the purpose of which was to urge citizens to communicate in a more respectful and effective way—not to end disagreement, but to improve public discourse by reminding people of the very basic principles of respect.

Now therefore, be it resolved by the Common Council of the City of Superior, Wisconsin, that the Superior City Council recognizes nine tools of civility that will provide increased opportunities for civil discourse in order to find positive resolutions to the issues that face our city. These tools include:

1. Pay attention.
2. Listen.
3. Be inclusive.
4. Don't gossip.
5. Show respect.
6. Be agreeable.
7. Apologize.
8. Give constructive criticism.
9. Take responsibility.
10. *Tell the truth (*Amended at the 9/2/03 Council meeting).

Be it further resolved, that the Superior City Council shall promote the use and adherence of these tools in conducting the business of the Council.

www.ci.superior.wi.us

NOTES

Chapter 1

1   Fletcher, E. (June 25, 2009). "Stung by Sacha Baron Cohen: Borat's etiquette consultant," *The Daily Telegraph*, retrieved on August 5, 2010, from http://www.telegraph.co.uk/culture/sacha-baron-cohen/5603060/Stung-by-Sacha-Borats-etiquette-consultant.html.

2   Bozell Worldwide/US News & World Report Civility in America Study, 1999.

3   Public Agenda Research Group, April 3, 2002, reported on ABCNews.com.

4   Grier, P. (September 14, 2009). "What can house do to Joe Wilson for 'You Lie' outburst?," *The Christian Science Monitor*, retrieved on August 5, 2010, from http://www.csmonitor.com/USA/Politics/2009/0914/ what-can-house-do-to-joe-wilson-for-you-lie-outburst.

5   Forni, P.M. (2002). *Choosing civility: The twenty-five rules of considerate conduct*. New York: St. Martin's Griffin.

6   Carter, S. (1998). *Civility: manners, morals, and the etiquette of democracy.* New York: Basic Books.

7   *Webster's Third International Dictionary*. (June 2002). Springfield: Merriam-Webster.

8   Forni, *supra* note 5, at 7-8.

9   *Id.* at 9.

10   *Id.* at 12, also see Random House *Webster's Unabridged Dictionary* (2001). New York: Random House Reference and Information Publishing.

11   The Revised Standard Version of the Bible, Matthew 22:39.

12   *Forni, supra note 5, at 48-53.*

13   *Ibid. at 35.*

14   *Webster's Third, supra* note 7.

15   Strauss, W. and Howe, N. (1991). *Generations: The history of America's future, 1584 to 2069.* New York: Harper Perennial.

16   Calvert, C. and Richards, R. D. (2004). "Fans and the First Amendment: Cheering and jeering in college sports," 4 *Virginia Sports & Entertainment Law Journal* 1.

17   The Ohio State University Task Force on Preventing Celebratory Riots, Final Report. (April 7, 2003). Retrieved on September 9, 2010, from http://ehe.osu.edu/taskforce/downloads/finalreport.pdf.

18   Lombardi, K. and Jones, K. (December 3, 2009). "Campus sexual assault statistics don't add up," *The Center for Public Integrity,* retrieved on September 9, 2010, from http://www.publicintegrity.org/ investigations/campus_assault/articles/entry/1841/.

19   Hauser, C. (April 16, 2007). "Virginia Tech shootings leave 33 dead," *The New York Times,* retrieved on October 26, 2010, from http://www.nytimes.com/2007/04/16/us/16cnd-shooting.html.

20   Jackson, B. (1991). "The Lingering Legacy of In Loco Parentis: An Historical Survey and Proposal for Reform," 44 *Vanderbilt Law Review* 1135, 1136.

21   *Id.*

22   *Id.* at 1136 n.4.

23   Starr, K. (2009). "From Fraser to Frederick: Bong hits and the decline of civil culture," 42 *University of California Davis Law Review* 661 (quoting Lottie H. Kendzierski, Aristotle and Pagan Education, in Some Philosophers on Education: Papers Concerning the Doctrines of Augustine, Aristotle, Aquinas & Dewey 26, 27 (Donald A. Gallagher ed., 1956))

24   Aristotle, (2007). *The Nicomachean Ethics.* Minneapolis: Filiquarian Publishing.

25   Milson, A. J. (2005). *Reading in American educational thought: From puritanism to progressivism,* at 91, 105. Greenwich: Information Age Publishing.

26   Brubacher, J. and Rudy, W. (3d ed. 1976). *Higher education in transition: A history of American colleges and universities,* 177-80. New Jersey: Transaction Publishers.

27   Jackson, *supra* note 19, at 1141-44.

28   Starr, *supra* note 22, at 668-69 (referring to *Tinker v. Des Moines Independent Community School District,* 393 U.S. 503 (1969)).

29   The Supreme Court most recently dealt with the issue of student free speech in *Morse v. Frederick,* 551 U.S. 393 (2007). In *Morse,* the Court produced a very narrow holding: high school administrators could "restrict student speech at a school event, when that speech is reasonably viewed as promoting illegal drug use." But as noted by Ken Starr, only Justice Thomas gave any credence to the view that educators have a duty to instill moral virtue in their students as a countervailing rationale to the Court's First Amendment jurisprudence. Starr, *supra* note 22, at 674-77.

30   Huntley, R. (2006). *The world according to Y: Inside the new adult generation.* Sydney: Allen & Unwin.

31   The Pew Research Center. (January 9, 2007). "How young people view their lives, futures, and politics: a portrait of 'generation next'," retrieved on September 9, 2010, from http://people-press.org/reports/pdf/300.pdf.

32   Strauss and Howe, *supra* note 15.

33   Leung, R. (September 4, 2005). "The echo-boomers," *60 Minutes,* retrieved on September 9, 2010, from http://www.cbsnews.com/stories/2004/10/01/60minutes/main646890.shtml.

34   Arhin, A. O. and Johnson-Mallard, V. (Nov-Dec 2003). "Encouraging alternative forms of self expression in the generation Y student: A strategy for effective learning

in the classroom," *The ABNF Journal*, retrieved on September 9, 2010, from http://findarticles.com/p/articles/mi_m0MJT/is_6_14/ ai_112905386/?tag=untagged.

35   Strauss and Howe, *supra* note 15.

36   Nielsen Report. (June 2009). "How teens use media," retrieved on September 9, 2010, from http://blog.nielsen.com/nielsenwire/reports/nielsen_howteensusemedia_june09.pdf, at p.9.

37   Pryor, J. H., Hurtado, S., Sharkness, J., et al. (2008). "The American freshman: National norms for fall 2008," University of California at Los Angeles Higher Education Research Institute, retrieved on September 9, 2010, from http://www.heri.ucla.edu/pr-display.php?prQry=28.

38   The Pew Research Center for the People and the Press. (January 9, 2007). "How young people view their lives, futures and politics: A portrait of 'generation next'," retrieved on October 26, 2010, from http://people-press.org/pdf/300.pdf.

39   Huntley, *supra* note 30; Strauss and Howe, *supra* note 15.

40   Hira, N. A. (May 15, 2007). "Attracting the twentysomething worker," *CNNMoney.com*, retrieved on September 9, 2010, from http://money.cnn.com/magazines/fortune/fortune_archive /2007/05/28/100033934/

Chapter 2

1   DeSantis, A. D. (2007). *Inside Greek U.: Fraternities, sororities, and the pursuit of pleasure, power, and prestige*, at 6. Lexington: University Press of Kentucky.

2   Forni, P.M. (2002). *Choosing civility: The twenty-five rules of considerate conduct*, at 12. New York: St. Martin's Griffin.

3   WhyGoGreek.com. Statistics about Greek Life. Retrieved on September 9, 2010, www.whygogreek.com/stats.html.

4   DeSantis, *supra* note 1.

5   National Institute on Alcohol Abuse and Alcoholism. (2002). "A call to action: Changing the culture of drinking at U.S. colleges," retrieved on September 9, 2010, from http://www.collegedrinkingprevention. gov/niaaacollegematerials/taskforce/taskforce_toc.aspx.

6   Harvard School of Public Heath, College Alcohol Study, available at http://www.hsph.harvard.edu/cas.

7   *Id.*

8   *Id.*

9   DeSantis, *supra* note 1, at 7-8.

10   Lewis, K. M. and Rice, T. W. (Oct. 2005). "Voter turnout in undergraduate student government elections," 38 *PS: Political Science and Politics* 723, 729.

11   Winston, R. B., Nettles, III, W. R. and Opper, Jr., J. H., eds. (1987). *Fraternities and Sororities on the Contemporary College Campus*. San Francisco: Jossey-Bass.

12   Ferguson, C. W. (1937). *Fifty million brothers*, at 40. New York: Farrar & Rinehart.

13   DeSantis, *supra* note 1, at 4.

14   Ross, L.C. (2000). *The divine nine: The history of African American fraternities and sororities*. New York: Kensington.

15   DeSantis, *supra* note 1, at 5.

16   Center for the Study of the College Fraternity, Frequently Asked Questions Web page, retrieved on May 26, 2010, from http://www.indiana.edu/~cscf/faq.htm.

17   Robins, A. (2004). *Pledged: The Secret Life of Sororities*. New York: Hyperion.

18   Dillon, S. (February 26, 2007). "Sorority evictions raise messy issue of looks and bias," *The New York Times*, retrieved September 9, 2010, from http://www.nytimes.com/2007/02/25/education/ 25sorority.html.

19   Allen, E. J. and Madden, M. (March 11, 2008). "Hazing in view: College students at risk," *National Study of Student Hazing*, retrieved on September 9, 2010, from www.hazingstudy.org/publications/hazing_in_ view_web.pdf.

20   *Id.*

21   Lipka, S. (March 21, 2008). "Student-affairs meeting: Hazing extends beyond fraternities: What parents expect," 54 *The Chronicle of Higher Education* 28(A21).

22   HazingPrevention.org. Statistics, retrieved on September 10, 2010, from http://www.hazingprevention.org/page.php?page_id=21927.

23   Allen and Madden, *supra* note 19.

24   Korry, E. (November 14, 2005). "A fraternity hazing gone wrong," National Public Radio, retrieved on September 9, 2010, from http://www.npr.org/templates/story/story.php?storyId=5012154.

25   *Id.*

26   *Id.*

27   Lipka, *supra* note 21, citing NASPA Study.

28   The Higher Education Center for Alcohol and Drug Abuse and Violence Prevention. (August 2008). "Fraternity and Sorority Members and Alcohol and Other Drug Use," retrieved on September 10, 2010, from http://www.higheredcenter.org/files/product/fact_sheet5.pdf.

29   Ferrell, E. F. (February 24, 2006). "Putting fraternities in their place," 52 *The Chronicle of Higher Education* 25(A34).

Chapter 3

1   U.S. Census Bureau. (October 2008). "School enrollment—social and economic characteristics of students," Table 5, retrieved on September 9, 2010, from http://www.census.gov/population/www/socdemo/school/cps2008.html.

2   Center for Academic Integrity. (2005). "In new CAI research conducted by Don McCabe levels of cheating and plagiarism remain high," retrieved on September 9, 2010, from https://secure2.mc.duke.edu/academicintegrity/cai_research.asp.

3   *Id.*

4   Callahan, D. (2006). "On campus: Author discusses the 'cheating culture' with college students," *Plagiary* 1(4): 1-8.

5   Stuber-McEwen, D., Wiseley, P. and Hoggatt, S. (Fall 2009). "Point, click, and cheat: Frequency and type of academic dishonesty in the virtual classroom," *Online Journal*

of Distance Learning and Administration, retrieved on September 9, 2010, from http://www.westga.edu/~distance/ojdla/fall123/stuber123.html.

6   Storch, E. A. and Storch, J. B. (2003). "Academic dishonesty and attitudes towards academic dishonest acts: Support for cognitive dissonance theory," 92 *Psychological Reports* 174-177.

7   Stuber-McEwen, Wiseley, and Hoggatt, *supra* note 5.

8   Baker, R. K., Berry, P. and Thornton, B. (2008). "Attitudes on academic integrity violations," 5 *Journal of College Teaching & Learning* 5-13.

9   Weeks, K. M. (Spring 2007). "Academic dishonesty," 30 *Lex Collegii* 4.

10   Young, J. R. (April 2, 2010). "High-tech cheating on homework abounds, and professors look away," *The Chronicle of Higher Education* A (14).

11   *Id.*

12   Rimer, S. (September 3, 2003). "A campus fad that's being copied: Internet plagiarism seems on the rise," *The New York Times*, retrieved on September 9, 2010, from http://www.nytimes.com/2003/09/03/nyregion/a-campus-fad-that-s-being-copied-internet-plagiarism-seems-on-the-rise.html.

13   *Id.*

14   *Id.*

15   *Black's Law Dictionary* (6th ed. 1990).

16   Maurer, H., Kappe, F., and Zaka, B. (2006). "Plagiarism—A Survey," 12 *Journal of Universal Computer Science* 8. *Also see* The Center for Academic Integrity's Assessment Project Research Survey by Don McCabe, available at http://www.academicintegrity.org/cai_research/index.php.

17   *Id.*

18   Center for Academic Integrity, *supra* note 2.

19   Weeks, *supra* note 9.

20   Stuber-McEwen, Wiseley, and Hoggatt, *supra* note 5.

21   American Association of University Professors. (9th Ed. 2001). *Policy Documents and Reports.* AAUP: Washington, DC.

22   *Id.* See "Joint Statement on Rights and Freedoms of Students."

23   *Id.*

24   Marklein, M. B. (June 18, 2009). "Colleges strive to ensure intellectual diversity," *USAToday.com*, retrieved on September 10, 2010, from http://www.usatoday.com/news/education/2009-06-17-college-free-speech_N.htm.

25   Horowitz, D. (February 13, 2004). "In defense of intellectual diversity," 50 *The Chronicle of Higher Education* 23, B12.

26   Weeks, K. M. (Spring 2006). "Student Civility," 29 *Lex Collegii* 4.

27   U.S.C. Student Judicial Affairs and Community Standards, *Disruptive Classroom Behavior*, retrieved on September 9, 2010, from www.usc.edu/student-affairs/SJACS/disruptive.html.

28   Weeks, *supra* note 26.

29   Respect and Civility in the Campus Community, University of California, Berkeley, retrieved on September 9, 2010, from http://students.berkeley.edu/uga/respect.stm.

Chapter 4

1   McCormick, A. C. and McCormick, R. A. (2008). "The emperor's new clothes: Lifting the NCAA's veil of amateurism," 45 *San Diego Law Review* 495, 496.

2   Lewis, G. (1970). "The beginning of organized college sport," 22 *American Quarterly* 222, 223.

3   *Id.*

4   Carter, W. B. (2006). "The Age of Innocence: The First Twenty-Five Years of the National Collegiate Athletics Association, 1906-1931," 8 *Vanderbilt Journal of Entertainment Law* 211, 215.

5   Trosclair, C. (August 29, 2009). "College football attendance in a recession: Major teams played to record crowds in 2008, small schools suffered," *Suite 101 Online Newspaper*, retrieved on September 10, 2010, from http://college-football.suite101. com/article.cfm/recession_impact_on_college_football _attendance.

6   Learmonth, M. (April 17, 2008). "CBS: March madness eyeballs worth more on web than TV," *Business Insider*, retrieved on September 10, 2010, from http://www. businessinsider.com/2008/4/cbs-online-viewers-worth-more-than-tv.

7   McEvoy, C. (Fall 2005). "The relationship between dramatic changes in team performance and undergraduate admissions applications," 2 *The Sports Magazine and Related Topics Journal* 1 retrieved on October 5, 2010, from http://www.thesmartjournal. com/admissions.pdf.

8   Schultz, M. (April 23, 2007). "Athletes are pumping up Adrian College enrollment," *The Detroit News* retrieved on September 10, 2010, from http://detnews.com/ article/20070423/SCHOOLS/704230366.

9   *Simpson v. Univ. of Col. Boulder*, 500 F.3d 1170 (10th Cir. 2007).

10   Suggs, W. (February 22, 2002). "NCAA gets tough on rule violators, after several years of light penalties," *The Chronicle of Higher Education* A33.

11   *Simpson v. Univ. of Col. Boulder, supra* note 9 at 1180.

12   *Id.* at 1184.

13   Nelson, T. F and Wechsler, H. (2001). "Alcohol and college athletes," 33(1) *Medicine and Science in Sports and Exercise* 43-47. *See also* The Higher Education Center for Alcohol and Other Drug Abuse and Violence Protection. (August 2008). "College athletes and alcohol and other drug use," retrieved on September 10, 2010, from http:// www.higheredcenter.org/files/product/fact_sheet3.pdf.

14   Lombardi, K. (February 24, 2010). "A lack of consequences for sexual assault," *The Center for Integrity*, retrieved on September 10, 2010, from http://www.publicintegrity. org/investigations/campus_assault/ articles/entry/1945/.

15   National Collegiate Athletic Association. (August 1, 2008). *NCAA Division I Manual*. Indianapolis: NCAA. See Bylaw 14.4. Retrieved on September 10, 2010, from http:// www.ncaapublications.com/ productdownloads/D109.pdf.

16   Wolverton, B., Kelderman, E., and Moser, K. (September 5, 2008). "Spending plenty so athletes can make the grade," 55 *Chronicle of Higher Education* Issue 2 at page A1.

17   Thamel, P. (July 13, 2006). "For some athletes, courses with no classes," *The New York Times*, retrieved on September 10, 2010, from http://www.nytimes.com/2006/07/13/sports/13cnd-auburn.html.

18   Weiberg, S. (Nov. 21, 2005). "Colleges are reaching their limit on alcohol," *USA Today*, retrieved on September 10 from http://www.usatoday.com/sports/college/2005-11-16-colleges-alcohol_x.htm.

19   Toben F. Nelson and Henry Wechsler, Ph.D., Harvard School of Public Health College and Alcohol Study.

20   National Collegiate Athletic Association. Football Attendance Statistics, retrieved on September 10, 2010, from http://www.ncaa.org/wps/wcm/connect/public/ncaa/resources/stats/football/ attendance/index.html.

21   National Collegiate Athletic Association. (2009). 2009 National College Basketball Attendance (For All NCAA Men's Varsity Teams), retrieved on September 10, 2010, from http://web1.ncaa.org/web_files/ stats/m_basketball_RB/Reports/2009mbbattend.pdf.

22   Whal, G. (March 3, 2008). "Over the top," *Sports Illustrated*, retrieved on September 10, 2010, from http://sportsillustrated.cnn.com/vault/article/magazine/MAG1109807/index/index.htm.

23   Wasserman, H. M. (2004). "*Fan Profanity*," *First Amendment Center*, retrieved on September 10, 2010, from http://www.firstamendmentcenter.org/speech/pubcollege/topic.aspx?topic=fan_profanity ("Fans have created controversy by targeting a player whose girlfriend had posed in Playboy, chanting 'rapist' at a player who had pled guilty to sexual assault and waving fake joints at a player with a history of drug use.").

24   Wahl, *supra* note 22.

25   The Associated Press. (February 2, 2010). "Rowdy West Virginia student section under fire," *NBC Sports*, retrieved on September 10, 2010, from http://nbcsports.msnbc.com/id/35205635/ns/sports-college_basketball. Also see http://www.youtube.com/watch?v=UGGmBpTiETw.

26   Rains, B. J. (Sept. 9, 2008). "Athletics dept. wants to get that $*@#ing chant out," *The University Daily Kansan Online*, retrieved on September 10, 2010, from http://www.kansan.com/news/2008 /sep/09/chant/.

27   Wahl, *supra* note 22.

28   Rains, *supra* note 26.

29   Zapotosky, M. (March 5, 2010). "Unruly revelry after Maryland game leads to 28 arrests in College Park," *The Washington Post* at B01.

30   Rees, D. I. and Schnepel, K. T. (January 2008). "College football games and crime," Cornell Working Paper Series No. 08-01.

31   *Id.*

32   Associated Press. (April 13, 2003). "Fans turn violent after hockey game," *CBS College Sports*, retrieved on September 10, 2010, from http://www.cstv.com/sports/m-hockey/stories/041203aad.html.

33   Suggs, W. (March 7, 2003). "College Officials Discuss How to Stop Mayhem After Big Games," 49 *Chronicle of Higher Education* at A43.

34   Rees and Schnepel, *supra* note 30.

Chapter 5

1   United States Census Bureau. (2008). "Characteristics of the Group Quarters Population by Group Quarters Type," Chart S2601B, retrieved on September 10, 2010, from http://factfinder.census.gov/servlet/STTable?_bm=y&-qr_name=ACS_2008_3YR_G00_S2601B&-geo_id=01000US&-ds_name=ACS_2008_3YR_G00_&-_lang=en&-redoLog=false [Opener: number of people living in on-campus college housing.]

2   Hoover, E. (Aug. 8, 2008). "Campuses See Rising Demand for Housing," 54 *Chronicle of Higher Education* Issue 47, at pp. A1, A15.

3   Read, B. and Young, J. R. (August 4, 2006). Facebook and other social-networking sites raise questions for administrators. 48 *The Chronicle of Higher Education* 48, A29.

4   Farrell, E. F. (September 1, 2006). "Judging roommates by their Facebook cover," 53 *The Chronicle of Higher Education* Issue 2, A63.

5   Blimling, G. S. and Miltenberger, L. (1981). *The Resident Assistant.* Dubuque: Kendall/Hunt Publishing Company.

6   *Id.*

7   Jackson, B. (1991). "The Lingering Legacy of In Loco Parentis: An Historical Survey and Proposal for Reform," 44 *Vanderbilt Law Review* 1135, 1136.

8   Meyer, W. B. (December 2004). "Harvard and heating the revolution," 77 *The New England Quarterly* 4, pp. 588-606.

9   Supiano, B. (2008). "Swankier suites, more students?," 54 *Chronicle of Higher Education* 31, pA1-A25; *see also* http://www.time.com/time/photogallery/0,29307,1838306_1759869,00.html.

10   Biemiller, L. (2009). "More community colleges build residence halls," 55 *Chronicle of Higher Education* 33, pA19-A19. (Even some community colleges have looked at the possibility of adding permanent student residences.).

11   Biemiller, L. (2007). "The dorm room of the future," 53 *Chronicle of Higher Education* 25, p B12-B13.

12   Emerson, R. M. (September 2008). "Responding to roommate troubles: Reconsidering informal dyadic control," 42 *Law and Society Review* 483.

13   Lipka, S. (2008). "Matchmaker, matchmaker, find me a roommate," 55 *Chronicle of Higher Education* 3, p A1-A8.

14   Mytelka, A. (September 20, 2008) "U. of Arizona student convicted of killing roommate," *The Chronicle of Higher Education.*

15   Fee, S. (2005). *My roommate is driving me crazy! Solve conflicts, set boundaries, and survive the college roommate from hell.* Avon: Adams Media.

16   Forni, P.M. (2009). *The civility solution: What to do when people are rude.* New York: St. Martin's Griffin.

17   Anderson Analytics. (December 8, 2009). "College students say Facebook is only social network site that really matters." Survey of College Student Media Consumption, retrieved on September 10, 2010, from http://www.andersonanalytics.com/index.php?mact=News,cntnt01,detail,0&cntnt01articleid=72&cntnt01origid=16&cntnt01detailtemplate=newsdetail.tpl&cntnt01dateformat=%25m.%25d.%25Y&cntnt01returnid=46.

18   Dionne, E. H. (2008). "Pornography, morality, and harm: Why Miller should survive Lawrence," 15 *George Mason Law Review* 611, 622 citing Paul, P. (2005). *Pornified: How Pornography Is Transforming Our Lives, Our Relationships, and Our Families.* New York: Times Books; *see also* Carr, J. L. and VanDeusen, K. M. (2004). "Risk Factors for Male Sexual Aggression on College Campuses," 19 *Journal of Family Violence* 279, 284 (reporting that at least 42% of college men surveyed in a 1999 survey consumed pornography); Durham, M. G. (2009). "X-Rated America," 55 *Chronicle of Higher Education* 18, pB14-B15; http://www.insidehighered.com/news/2009/04/03/pornography.

19   *Miller v. California,* 413 U.S. 15 (1973).

20   *Brockett v. Spokane Arcades, Inc.,* 472 U.S. 491, 498 (1985).

21   Oldenkamp, E. (1997). "Pornography, the Internet, and student-to-student sexual harassment: A dilemma resolved with Title VII and Title IX," 162 *Duke Journal of Gender Law and Policy* 4:159.

22   O'Neil, R. (March 21, 2003). "What limits should campus networks place on pornography?," 49 *The Chronicle of Higher Education* 28, B20.

23   Ferguson, C. J., (June 22, 2007). "Video games: The latest scapegoat for violence," 53 *Chronicle of Higher Education* 42, B20.

24   Read, B. (2006). "Piracy and copyright: An ethics lesson," 52 *Chronicle of Higher Education* 37, p. 46-50.

25   *Metro-Goldwyn-Mayer Studios, Inc. v. Grokster, Ltd,* 545 U.S. 913 (2005).

26   Weeks, K. M. (2007). *Managing Campus Cyberspace and the Law,* Nashville: College Legal Information.

27   Read, B. (March 16, 2007). "Record companies to accused pirates: Deal or no deal?," *Chronicle of Higher Education.*

28   Siwek, S. E. (Oct. 3, 2007). "The true costs of copyright industry piracy to the U.S. economy," *Institute for Policy Innovation Report* # 189, retrieved on September 10, 2010, from http://www.ipi.org/ipi%5CIPI Publications.nsf/PublicationLookupF ullTextPDF/02DA0B4B44F2AE9286257369005ACB57/$File/CopyrightPiracy. pdf?OpenElement.

29   Recording Institute of America Website, Frequently Asked Questions, retrieved on May 31, 2010, from www.riaa.com/faq.php.

30   *Id.*

31   *Id.*

Chapter 6

1   Of course, there are examples of behaviors that are arguably self-destructive but provide benefits for others. For instance, choosing to do volunteer work in developing nations with unsafe or unhealthy living conditions isn't a *healthy* choice, but it is one that provides a significant benefit to others.

2   National Institute on Alcohol Abuse and Alcoholism. (2002). "High-risk drinking in college: What we know and what we need to learn," U.S. Department of Health and Human Services, Washington, DC.

3   Capone, C., Wood, M. D., Borsari, B. and Laird, R. D. (September 2007). "Fraternity and sorority involvement, social influences, and alcohol use among college students: A prospective examination," 21(3) *Psychology of Addictive Behavior* 316.

4   Hingson, R., Heeren, T., Winter, M., and Wechsler, H. (2005). "Magnitude of alcohol-related mortality and morbidity among U.S. college students ages 18-24: Changes from 1998 to 2001," *Annual Review of Public Health* 26:259-279; also see http://www. collegedrinkingprevention.gov/statssummaries /snapshot.aspx.

5   Leinwand, Donna. (March 15, 2007). "College drug use, binge drinking rise," *USA Today*, retrieved on September 10, 2010, from http://www.usatoday.com/news/ nation/2007-03-15-college-drug-use_N.htm.

6   Capone, Wood, Borsari, and Laird, *supra* note 3.

7   National Institute on Alcohol Abuse and Alcoholism. (April 2002). "High-risk drinking in college: What we know and what we need to learn," *College Drinking Prevention,* retrieved on September 10, 2010, from http://www.collegedrinkingprevention.gov/ media/FINALPanel1.pdf.

8   Wechsler, H., Eun Lee, J., Kuo, M., Seibring, M., Nelson, T.B., and Lee, H. (April 2002). "Trends in college binge drinking during a period of increased prevention efforts: Findings from 4 *Harvard School of Public Health College Alcohol Surveys*: 1993-2001." *Journal of American College Health*; 50:203-217.

9   Meilman, P. W.; Leichliter, J. S.; and Presley, C. A. (1999). "Greeks and athletes: Who drinks more?" 47 *Journal of American College Health* 187-190.

10   Capone, Wood, Borsari, and Laird, *supra* note 3.

11   *Id.*

12   Johnston, L. D., O'Malley, P. M., Bachman, J. G., & Schulenberg, J. E. (2008). *Monitoring the Future national survey results on drug use, 1975-2007. Volume II: College students and adults ages 19-45* (NIH Publication No. 08-6418B). Bethesda, MD: National Institute on Drug Abuse, 319 pp., retrieved on September 10, 2010, from http://monitoringthefuture.org/pubs/monographs/vol2_2007.pdf.

13   The Higher Education Center for Alcohol and Other Drug Abuse and Violence Prevention. (August 2008). "Marijuana use among students at institutions of higher education," retrieved on September 10, 2010, from http://www.higheredcenter.org/ files/product/marijuana.pdf.

14   *Id.* Also see WeDontServeTeens.com, Dangers, retrieved on September 10, 2010, from www.dontserveteens.gov/dangers.html.

15   *Id.*

16   The Higher Education Center for Alcohol and Other Drug Abuse and Violence Prevention, *supra* note 13.

17   *Id.*

18   Marijuana Addiction Treatment, retrieved on September 10, 2010, from http://www. marijuanaaddictiontreatment.org/statistics-facts.html.

19   National Eating Disorder Association. (2004). "What causes eating disorders," retrieved on September 10, 2010, from http://www.nationaleatingdisorders.org/nedaDir/files/ documents/ handouts/WhatCaus.pdf.

20   Ferrell, E. F. (July 12, 2002). "Students won't give up their French fries," *The Chronicle of Higher Education* A35.

21   The American Foundation for Suicide Prevention. Facts and Figures, retrieved on September 10, 2010, from http://www.afsp.org/index.cfm?fuseaction=home. viewpage&page_id=050CDCA2-C158-FBAC-16ACCE9DC8B7026C.

22   National Institute of Mental Health. *Depression*, retrieved on September 10, 2010, from http://www.nimh.nih.gov/health/publications/depression/complete-index.shtml, also see http://www.med.umich.edu/opm/newspage/2003/collegedepression.htm.

23   *Id.*

24   Tsuang, M. T. and Faraone, S. V. (1990). *The genetics of mood disorders*, Baltimore: Johns Hopkins University Press; also see Tsuang, M. T., Bar, J. L., Stone, W. S., and Faraone, S. V. (June 2004). "Gene environment interactions in mental disorders," 3(2) *World Psychiatry* 73-83.

25   Gavin, K. "Heading back to campus? Watch for depression triggered by college stresses, U-M expert advises," (August 4, 2003), retrieved on September 10, 2010, from http://www.med.umich.edu/opm/newspage/2003/collegedepression.htm.

26   *Id.*

27   National Institute of Mental Health, *supra* note 22.

28   Kadison, R. D. (December 10, 2004). "The mental-health crisis: What colleges must do," 51 *Chronicle of Higher Education* 16(B20).

29   Centers for Disease Control and Prevention. National Center for Injury Prevention and Control. Web-Based Injury Statistics Query and Reporting System (WISQARS): www.cdc.ncipc/wisqars.

30   JED Foundation, http://www.jedfoundation.org/professionals; also see National Institute of Mental Health, "Suicide in the U.S.: Statistics and Prevention" available at http://www.nimh.nih.gov/health/publications/suicide-in-the-us-statistics-and-prevention/index.shtml.

31   The American Foundation for Suicide Prevention, *supra* note 21.

32   Gavin, *supra* note 25.

33   Bogle, K. A. (March 21, 2008). "Hooking up: What educators need to know," 54 *Chronicle of Higher Education* 28 (A32).

34   Bogle, K. A. (August 11, 2007). "Hooking up and the sexual double standard among college students," *Paper presented at the annual meeting of the American Sociological Association*, TBA, New York, New York City, available at www.allacademic.com/meta/p184479_index.html.

35   *Id.*

36   Weeks, K. M. and Gilkes, E. E. (2010). "Sexual assault or hooking up?," 33 *Lex Collegii* 4.

37   Associated Press. (August 17, 2010). "Love makes teen sex less academically harmful, study says," *CNN Living*, retrieved on September 8, 2010, from http://articles.cnn.com/2010-08-17/living/teen.sex.school_1_dropouts-sexual-activity-relationships?_s=PM:LIVING.

38   Bogle, *supra* note 33.

Chapter 7

1   Gurin, P., Bowen, W. et al. (January 1999). "The Compelling Need for Diversity in Higher Education." Expert reports prepared from *Gratz et al. v. Bollinger, et al.* No. 97-75231 (E.D. Mich.) and *Grutter, et al. v. Bollinger, et al.* No. 97-75928 (E.D. Mich.). Retrieved on July 30, 2010 from http://www.vpcomm.umich.edu/admissions/research/.

2   Tajfel, H. (1981). *Human groups and social categories: Studies in social psychology.* Cambridge, England: Cambridge University Press.

3   Billig, M. (1985). "Prejudice, categorization, and particularization: From a perceptual to a rhetorical approach." *European Journal of Social Psychology*, 15, 79-103.

4   Allport, G. (1954). *The Nature of Prejudice.* Reading, MA: Addison-Wesley.

5   Islam, M. R. and Hewstone, M. (1993). Dimensions of contact as predictors of intergroup anxiety, perceived out-group variability, and out-group attitude: An integrative model. *Personality and Social Psychology Bulletin, 19,* 700-710.

6   Entman, R. M., & Rojecki, A. (2000). The Black image in the white mind: Media and race in America. Chicago, IL: University of Chicago Press.

7   Williams, D. A. and Wade-Golden, K. C. (Sept. 26, 2008). "The complex mandate of a chief diversity officer," 55 *Chronicle of Higher Education* 5, B44.

8   Saad, L. (May 29, 2007). "Tolerance for gay rights at high-water mark," *Gallup News Service*, retrieved on August 24, 2010, from http://www.gallup.com/poll/27694/tolerance-gay-rights-highwater-mark.aspx.

9   Weeks, K. W. and Gilkes, E. E. (2010). "The new face of diversity: Transgender students and employees," 34 *Lex Collegii* 1.

10   Gurin, *supra* note 1.

11   *Id.*

12   Gurin, P. (1997). "Theoretical foundations for the effect of diversity," Expert Report, retrieved on July 23, 2010, from http://www.vpcomm.umich.edu/admissions/legal/expert/theor.html.

13   Hinrichs, P. (March 10, 2009). "The effects of affirmative action bans on college enrollment, educational attainment, and the demographic composition of universities," *Georgetown Public Policy Institute*, retrieved on August 25, 2010, from http://www9.georgetown.edu/faculty/plh24/hinrichs_aff_action.pdf.

14   *Regents of the University of California v. Bakke*, 438 U.S. 912 (1978).

15   *Gratz v. Bollinger*, 123 S.Ct. 2411 (2003).

16   *Id.* Also see *Grutter v. Bollinger*, 123 S.Ct. 2325 (2003).

Chapter 8

1   Weiss, Paul. (1941). *The Golden Rule, 38 Journal of Philosophy* 421, describing the universal appeal of the principle).

2   University of California at Los Angeles Higher Education Research Institute. (August 2009). "Attitudes and Characteristics of Freshmen at 4-Year Colleges, Fall 2008," published in *The Nation's Students,* 56 *Chronicle of Higher Education*, Issue 1, at 18 (Aug. 28, 2009) (reporting that 29.3 percent of entering college students in 2008 estimated that chances were "very good" that they would "Participate in volunteer or community-service work").

BIBLIOGRAPHY

Carter, Stephen L. *Civility: Manners, Morals, and the Etiquette of Democracy* (New York: Basic, 1998, 352 pages). Addresses a general audience.

Dahnke, Cassandra and Spath, Tomas *Reclaiming Civility in the Public Square: 10 Rules that Work,* (Livermore, CA: WingSpan Press, 2007, 130 pages). Addresses the needs to improve relationships in public and governmental areas.

Forni, P. M. *Choosing Civility: The Twenty-five Rules of Considerate Conduct* (New York: St. Martin's Press, 2002, 192 pages). Addresses a general audience and includes a list of rules, many of which have been adopted, at least in part, by campuses and local governments.

Forni, P. M. *The Civility Solution: What to Do When People Are Rude* (St. Martin's Press, 2008, 192 pages). Includes a general discussion of civility in personal behavior.

Richardson, Steven M., ed., *Promoting Civility: A Teaching Challenge* (San Francisco: Jossey-Bass Publishers, 1999, 100 pages). Examines the issues related to civility and classroom teaching.

BUY A SHARE OF THE FUTURE IN YOUR COMMUNITY

These certificates make great holiday, graduation and birthday gifts that can be personalized with the recipient's name. The cost of one S.H.A.R.E. or one square foot is $54.17. The personalized certificate is suitable for framing and will state the number of shares purchased and the amount of each share, as well as the recipient's name. The home that you participate in "building" will last for many years and will continue to grow in value.

Here is a sample SHARE certificate:

THIS CERTIFIES THAT

YOUR NAME HERE

HAS INVESTED IN A HOME FOR A DESERVING FAMILY

1985-2010

TWENTY-FIVE YEARS OF BUILDING FUTURES
IN OUR COMMUNITY ONE HOME AT A TIME

1200 SQUARE FOOT HOUSE @ $65,000 = $54.17 PER SQUARE FOOT
This certificate represents a tax deductible donation. It has no cash value.

YES, I WOULD LIKE TO HELP!

*I support the work that Habitat for Humanity does and I want to be part of the excitement! As a donor, I will receive periodic updates on your construction activities but, more importantly, I know my gift will help a family in our community realize the dream of homeownership. **I would like to SHARE in your efforts against substandard housing in my community!** (Please print below)*

PLEASE SEND ME _____ SHARES at $54.17 EACH = $ $_____

In Honor Of: _____

Occasion: (Circle One)   HOLIDAY   BIRTHDAY   ANNIVERSARY

          OTHER: _____

Address of Recipient: _____

Gift From: _____ *Donor Address:* _____

Donor Email: _____

I AM ENCLOSING A CHECK FOR $ $_____ PAYABLE TO HABITAT FOR HUMANITY OR PLEASE CHARGE MY VISA OR MASTERCARD (CIRCLE ONE)

Card Number _____ Expiration Date: _____

Name as it appears on Credit Card _____ Charge Amount $ _____

Signature _____

Billing Address _____

Telephone # Day _____ Eve _____

PLEASE NOTE: Your contribution is tax-deductible to the fullest extent allowed by law.
Habitat for Humanity • P.O. Box 1443 • Newport News, VA 23601 • 757-596-5553
www.HelpHabitatforHumanity.org

CPSIA information can be obtained at www.ICGtesting.com
Printed in the USA
LVOW111257070412

276617LV00001B/13/P